Ultimate
Serbian Cookbook

TOP 111 Serbian dishes that you can cook right now

By

Slavka Bodic

Ultimate Serbian Cookbook
TOP 111 Serbian dishes that you can cook right now
By
Slavka Bodic

Please sign up for free Balkan recipes:
www.balkanfood.org

Why this cookbook?

I was born in the Balkans, I used to live in the former Yugoslavia and I currently reside in Serbia. We never talked about food that much, since we were happy and good food was a normal part of our lives. After the fall of communism and dissolution of Yugoslavia, the Balkans became (yet again?) a place with negative associations for people around the globe. Some of them barely know where Croatia, Serbia, Macedonia, Kosovo, Bulgaria, or Turkey are, but they know that there is something wrong with that part of the world.

To my greatest regret, when I ask my friends from around the globe about something positive about Serbia or the region, they always mention only two things: Delicious food and nice people. "*I love your sarma,*" or, "*Your mom is preparing amazing musaka,*" are things I have heard so many times. I tried to present only recipes that our mothers have been making for decades, without adding "modern food." To be honest, I was smiling the whole time I was writing the recipes for two previous cookbooks and remembering so many nice moments while I was eating these 111 dishes. And *kajmak* and *ajvar* as well.

After quite unexpected success of two previous cookbooks, I decided to continue and share with you even more. I believe that sharing nice things with others is the most beautiful thing in the world. For me, the food I love and the recipes I like and develop are nice things I want to share. I hope you like this and other cookbooks that I am going to publish in the coming months.

Here, I will try to share with all of you my cooking secrets for all key Serbian dishes.

I'd be very grateful if you take the time to post a short review on Amazon.

Slavka Bodić

Table of Contents

ONE LAST THING 174

Introduction

I was the one and only child of my parents. I was also spoiled and a picky eater. I would play in a park near my home, and my mother would try to give me couple of morsels while I was playing around. Her cooking was the only cooking that I knew, and several from the list of the main dishes in this book belong to her. In this cookbook, I want to present traditional recipes and way of cooking.

Many recipes from internet exist in my home city, but not all ingredients are the same and the preparation is quite different. Even cousins within the same family prepare the same meal in different ways, adding some ingredients and skipping others. Meal preparation was often a big secret. Women often ask each other "*How do you make such a good...,* "and the response is always the same – "*I am not doing anything special, just adding a bit of...*"

With this cookbook, you will be able to make dishes like I do, like my mother does, and like my grandmother did. Similarly, like with my previous Balkan Cookbook and Mediterranean cookbook, I guarantee that all these meals are great and on an equal footing with any other world cuisine.

Serbia and the Balkans are well-known for its restaurants, but trying these dishes made by someone's mother is the real thing. Please, try to make these dishes a couple of times in order to "*feel the dish*" (quote by my grandmother). I really hope you smile while you prepare and consume our best meals!

Appetizers and Breakfast

Burek

Savory fillings baked in a thin pastry dough are popular throughout southern Europe, a legacy of the Ottoman Empire. They go by a variety of names — *börek, bourek, böreği, bouréki.* The best *burek* is in Bosnia and Herzegovina, but this pastry is quite popular in Serbia too.

Preparation Time: 40 minutes
Cooking Time: 60 minutes

Ingredients
Pastry
2 cups (460 gr) of flour
1/2 cup (120 ml) of warm water
1/4 cup (60 ml) of melted butter or olive oil
1 egg
Salt

Meat Filling
1 1/2 (680 gr) pounds of ground beef
3 onions
2 eggs
2 tablespoons of paprika
Salt and pepper
1/2 cup (120 gr) of melted butter or olive oil

Preparation
In a large bowl, use a wooden spoon to mix together the flour, warm water, melted butter or olive oil, egg, and salt until it combines in a doughy mass. Add more water, a tablespoon at a time, as needed to bring the ingredients together. Remove the dough to a floured work surface and knead until smooth and

pliable. Cover with plastic wrap and set aside to rest for at least 30 minutes. Preheat oven to 375°F (190°C). Mix together the ground beef, onions, eggs, paprika, salt and pepper in a large bowl until smooth and set aside.

Move the rested dough to a lightly floured work surface and roll out into a large rectangle. Place floured fists underneath the dough and gently pull sections of the dough out to form a very thin rectangle, about 2 feet by 3 feet (60 cm x 90 cm). Be careful not to tear holes in the dough. If you do, pinch them together. Let the dough rest for 10 minutes or so to dry out a little.

Brush the pastry dough all over with melted butter or olive oil. Place a row of the meat filling along the longer edge of the rolled out pastry dough, leaving a 1 inch (2,5 cm) border. Bring the bottom of the pastry up over the meat filling and roll it up into a long, sausage-shaped roll.

Lay one end of the roll onto the middle of a greased baking pan. Carefully wrap the remaining part of the pastry roll around itself to form a snail-shaped pie in the middle of the baking pan. Brush the top of the pastry with melted butter or olive oil. Place in the oven and bake for 35 to 45 minutes, or until cooked through and golden brown. Cut into wedges and serve with a large dollop of good yogurt.

BUREK VARIATIONS

Sirnica (Cheese burek):
Instead of meat, for the filling use a mixture of feta (1 pound) and ricotta (1/2 pound) cheese, 2 eggs and pepper.

Zeljanica (Spinach and cheese burek):
Instead of meat, for the filling use 2 pounds of frozen spinach, 1/2 pound feta cheese, 2 eggs, salt and pepper. Thaw the spinach and squeeze it dry before

mixing with the remaining ingredients or try using chopped sorrel in place of some of the spinach.

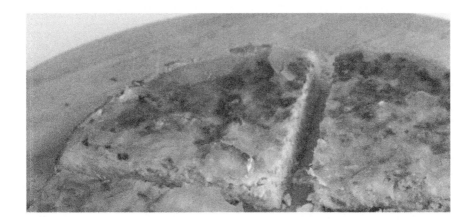

Gibanica

Gibanica is a pie or, better, the Queen of Pies. Once you taste it, you will make it again and again. Quite easy to prepare and it's a real, traditional food in Serbia.

Preparation Time: 20 minutes
Cooking Time: 50 minutes

Ingredients
1 pound (450 gr) of filo pastry
2/3 pound (300 gr) of cheese
2 small cups of oil
2 eggs
1 cup (240 ml) of sour cream
Some salt if the cheese isn't salty

Preparation
Whisk eggs with some sparkling water in a bowl, then add oil and crumbled cheese. Mix it well and add sour cream. Mix again. Oil the baking dish and line the sheets of filo pastry. First, put one layer of filo pastry at the bottom of the dish, then crumble two of them, dip them in the mixture and spread across the dish. Put one layer again, then spread two crumbled dipped ones and repeat until you run out of the mixture. Save one layer of pastry to put on top. Pour the remaining oil over the top layer. Bake in preheated oven on medium heat until golden brown.

Kachamak or Palenta

Kačamak or palenta, as it is also called, can be prepared in many ways. It's a real adventure to cook one! Whatever you may call it, you'll surely love this traditional Serbian meal made out of corn flour and water.

Preparation Time: 5 minutes
Cooking Time: 30 minutes

Ingredients

4 cups (960 ml) of water
2-3 teaspoons of salt
2/3 pound (300 gr) of corn flour (or polenta)
2 oz (60 gr) of butter (optional)

Preparation

Bring the water to boil in a large, heavy-based saucepan over high heat. Use a wire balloon whisk to stir the water. Gradually add the polenta in a thin, steady stream, whisking constantly until all the polenta is mixed into the water (whisking ensures for the polenta to be dispersed through the liquid as quickly as possible). Don't add the polenta too quickly or it will turn lumpy. Reduce the heat to low (cook the polenta on low heat, otherwise it will cook too quickly and you will need to add extra water). Simmer, stirring constantly with a wooden spoon for 10 minutes, or until the mixture thickens and the polenta is soft. (To test whether the polenta is soft or not, scoop a little of the polenta mixture onto a small plate and set aside to cool slightly. Rub the set aside polenta mixture between 2 fingers to see if the grains have softened. If the grains are still firm, continue to cook, stirring constantly over low heat, until the polenta is soft.) Remove from heat. Add cream and butter, and stir until well combined. Season to taste. Serve immediately with milk, yogurt, sour cream, or buttermilk over it.

Popara

Preparation Time: 10 minutes
Cooking Time: 30 minutes

Ingredients

1 1/3 pounds (600 gr) of homemade bread, baguettes or any crusty bread
¼ pound (120 gr) of feta cheese or Mozzarella cheese
4 tablespoons of butter
2 cups (480ml) of water
2 cups (480ml) of milk
Salt to taste

Preparation

Take a large saucepan, mix together the water, milk, and salt, and bring the mixture to a boil. When it starts to boil, add the bread broken in pieces, reduce heat, and cook till it softens up, about 3 minutes. Pour out extra water, you only need about 1 inch (2,5 cm) above bread line. Continue cooking for a few more minutes, mixing it gently on occasion. Then, add cheese and mix well. Serve on a plate with a teaspoon of butter on top of it.

Russian salad (*Ruska salata*)

Russian salad is ubiquitous in the Balkans and Eastern Europe, and has even made its way to as far as Argentina. In the region, this egg, veggie, meat and pickle salad, topped with mayo, is a holiday staple.

Preparation Time: 60 minutes

Ingredients

1 pound (450gr) of ham, sliced into fine cubes
An even amount of dill pickles, young sweet peas, carrots, and potatoes, all cooked carefully and cubed
1 pound (450gr) of mayonnaise
Salt and pepper to taste

Preparation

Boil carrots and potatoes until barely fork tender (watch carefully so the potatoes do not get too soft) and cool. Thaw frozen sweet young peas. Cut all vegetables (except peas) and ham to the same small sizes. Mix all ingredients together, except the mayonnaise. Add 2/3 pound (300 gr) of mayonnaise and salt and pepper and adjust each to taste. Chill for a few hours, or overnight, before serving.

Serbian Pandemonium salad (*Urnebes salata*)

Urnebes is a salad characteristic of Serbian cuisine, which originated in southern Serbia and is usually served as a side dish with barbecue. It should be very spicy; however, you can adjust the amounts to suit your own taste.

Preparation Time: 20 minutes

Ingredients
1 pound (450 gr) of feta cheese
½ cup (120 ml) of sour cream
3 large cloves of garlic, crushed
1½ teaspoons of sweet or hot paprika (or to taste)
1 - 2 teaspoons of dried chili flakes (or to taste)

Preparation
Crush the feta with a fork into a puree. Stir in sour cream to combine thoroughly with the feta. Add crushed garlic, paprika, and chili flakes. Mix well to combine. Garnish with additional paprika. Leave in the refrigerator overnight (the flavors will come together and develop during that time.)

Fried dough (*Uštipci*)

Different versions of uštipci exist everywhere in the region, and if you ever visit the Serbia, I am sure they will be offered to you at some point.

Preparation Time: 60 minutes
Cooking Time: 10 minutes

Ingredients

4 eggs
1 cup (240 ml) of sour cream
½ pound (230gr) of flour
1 sachet of baking powder
Salt
1 cup (240 ml) of oil

Preparation

Preparation and cooking of this fried dough without yeast takes about 20 minutes. It is served with white Serbian cream cheese or jam, with sour milk, regular milk, or tea. In a mixing bowl, break the eggs, mix them, add cream, mix more, and gradually pour in the flour with baking powder and salt. Continuing mixing until the dough is completely smooth. Leave it for about ten minutes to rest.

During this time, heat oil in a pan. Spoon drop the dough into the pan and bake at a moderate temperature. When fried dough becomes golden brown on all sides, remove them. Drop new dough and bake until the dough is gone. Serve warm.

Proja

Even today, proja is a "*guest*" at every Serbian dinner table and an integral part of every Serbian meze. Most modern projas, however, differ from the original, authentic proja. The original proja doesn't contain eggs, cheese, yogurt, or meat. It's made out of three basic ingredients: corn flour, salt and water.

Preparation Time: 10 minutes
Cooking Time: 40 minutes

Ingredients
5 cups (1,13kg) of corn flour
3 cups (680 gr) of flour
3 eggs
3 cups of oil
1 baking powder or baking soda
1 cup (240 ml) of yogurt
1 glass of mineral water
2 cups (460 gr) of cottage cheese

Preparation
Mix it all together and bake in a greased pan until golden. Cook for about 15-20 minutes at 450°F (230°C). It is best served with sour cream or buttermilk.

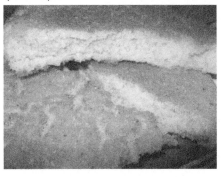

Roasted Red Pepper Sauce (*Ajvar*)

Ajvar (pronounced AYE-var) is a bright and robust red pepper relish that originates from the Balkans. Ajvar could be considered a sauce similar to ketchup in its tangy, slightly sweet flavor. Its most common use is as a topping for ćevapi sausages. Someone counted 196 versions of ajvar around the Balkans.

Cooking Time: 180 minutes

Ingredients

2 pounds (900 gr) of red bell peppers (about 5 medium peppers)

1 medium eggplant (about 3/4 pound)

5 teaspoons of freshly minced garlic (about 5 medium cloves)

1/4 cup (120 gr) of sunflower or olive oil

1 tablespoon of white vinegar

1 teaspoon of kosher salt

Freshly ground black pepper, to taste

Preparation

Light a chimney full of charcoal. When all the charcoals are lit and covered with gray ash, take out and arrange coals on one side of the charcoal grate. Set the cooking grate in place, cover the grill, and allow to preheat for 5 minutes. Clean and oil the grilling grate. Place peppers on the hot side of the grill and cook until blackened all over, 10-15 minutes. Transfer the peppers to a large bowl, cover with plastic wrap, and let sit until cool enough to handle, about 20 minutes. Remove charred skin, seeds, and cores from the peppers.

While the peppers are cooling, pierce the skin of an eggplant with a fork all over. Place the eggplant on cool side of the grill. Cover and cook until the skin darkens and wrinkles and the eggplant is uniformly soft when pressed with tongs, about 30 minutes, turning halfway through for even cooking. Remove the eggplant from the grill and let sit until cool enough to handle, about 10 minutes. Trim the top off the eggplant and split lengthwise. Using a spoon, scoop out the flesh of the eggplant, and discard the skin.

Place roasted red peppers, eggplant pulp, and garlic in a food processor fitted with a steel blade. Pulse until roughly chopped. Add in oil, vinegar and salt, and pulse until combined and peppers are finely chopped.

Transfer sauce to a medium saucepan. Bring to a simmer over medium-high heat, then reduce the heat to a medium-low and simmer for 30 minutes, stirring occasionally. Remove from heat and season with salt and pepper to taste. Let cool to room temperature, then use immediately or transfer to an airtight container and store in the refrigerator for up to two weeks.

Kajmak

Whether it's fresh and sweet or a little more "ripe" and salty, *kajmak* is a staple at Balkan tables. Citizens in this region make it a number of ways, but the best one is considered to be the one from west Serbia. Try to make it yourself! It is not a real *kajmak*, but it is the best version of it.

Preparation Time: 10 minutes

Ingredients
1/3 pound (150 gr) of butter
1/3 pound (150 gr) of hard feta cheese
1/3 pound (150 gr) of sour cream

Preparation
In a bowl, whisk the butter with a fork until it's fluffy. Add crumbled feta cheese and sour cream. Mix it all well. Note: You don't need to add salt to the *kajmak* as the feta cheese is salty on its own. If you like a milder *kajmak*, add some cream.

Poppy Seed Roll

Preparation time: 20 minutes
Cooking time: 100 minutes

Ingredients

Dough

3 1/3 cups of all-purpose flour
1 ¾ cups of lukewarm water
2 tablespoons of vegetable oil
1 tablespoon of orange marmalade
1 ½ oz of active yeast
1 tablespoon of sugar
A good pinch of salt

Filling

1 1/3 pounds of ground poppy seeds
6 tablespoons of sugar
Lemon zest of 1 lemon
2 ½ cups of milk

Preparation

Mix poppy seeds with 6 spoons of sugar, lemon zest, and milk. Cook the mixture on medium heat for 9-11 minutes, until it thickens up. When it's cooked, leave it to cool while you're preparing the dough. Mix yeast with 1 deciliter of lukewarm water and 1 tablespoon of sugar in a small bowl. Let it sit until the yeast starts to grow.

Sift flour into a bowl, but leave about 100 grams aside and add salt to the sifted flour. Pour yeast mixture into the flour and stir while adding the oil and the rest of the water to make dough. If it's too soft add more flour, until the consistency of bread dough. When it's combined start kneading it with your hands until it becomes smooth and silky. When dough is well kneaded, put it in a bowl, cover it with a cloth and put it in a warm place. When the dough expands and doubles in size, cut it in half.

Knead one half of the dough, and roll it into a rectangle. The width of the rectangle should be the length of the pan in which you'll be baking it. Spread half of the poppy seed filling over the rectangle, leaving a small border at the end. Roll the dough with poppies and place it in your baking pan. Repeat the same process with the other half of the dough and poppy mixture.

Mix marmalade with a spoon of water and use that to glaze the dough. Let the dough sit in the pan until it starts rising and then place it in a preheated oven to bake for about 40 minutes at 390 F. Baking time is around 30-40 minutes and it varies for different ovens. When the rolls become golden brown, remove them from the oven and cover with a kitchen towel until they are cool. Dust slices with icing sugar when serving.

Salty Cake with Black Toast Bread

Preparation time: 40 minutes

Ingredients

2 packs of black toast bread
1 ½ cups of sour cream
½ pound of ham
½ pound of cheese
2/3 pound of mayonnaise
4 pieces of boiled eggs
5 pieces of pickled gherkins
Salt to taste

Preparation

Prepare an appropriate tray to arrange this cake on. Make 3 different mixtures (fills) into the 3 separate containers. Make the first filling by mixing 100 g of mayonnaise, 80 g of sour cream, 250 g of finely chopped ham and 3 pickled gherkins cut or shredded to very small pieces.

Make the second filling by mixing ½ cup of mayonnaise, ½ cup of sour cream, 1 cup of grated cheese and 3 pieces of grated boiled eggs. Make the third (outer) filling by mixing ½ cup of mayonnaise and ½ cup of sour cream. Before the toast bread sorting on the tray, carefully cut and remove the outer toast bread crust. Sort the first layer of the black toast bread on a tray in a row, cover with the first filling. Put and arrange the second toast bread layer over the first filling, smear and spread the second (middle) filling. The third black toast bread layer goes on the top (over the second filling), which should be coated (the top and all sides) with the third filling mixture (mayonnaise and sour cream), sprinkled and decorated with 1/3 cup of finely grated cheese and 1 grated boiled egg.

Serbian Flatbread

Preparation time: 20 minutes
Cooking time: 100 minutes

Ingredients (12 servings)
1/4 oz package of active dry yeast
2 tablespoons of warm milk (115 degrees F)
1 cup of warm water (115 degrees F)
1 tablespoon of white sugar
2⅓ cups of all-purpose flour
1 teaspoon of salt

Preparation
Sprinkle the yeast over the warm milk in a small bowl. Let it sit for 5 minutes until the yeast softens and begins to form a creamy foam. Stir the sugar and warm water into the yeast mixture. Stir the flour and salt together in a separate bowl and add all but about 1/2 cup of the flour mixture to the yeast mixture. Mix with your hands until a soft dough forms, adding the last of the flour mixture a little at a time until it clears the sides of the bowl. Cover the bowl with a light cloth and let the dough rise in a warm place (80 to 95 F) until doubled in volume, about 1 hour.

Deflate, or 'punch down,' the dough and remove onto a work surface lightly dusted with flour and knead for about 5 minutes. Return the dough to the bowl, cover again with a light cloth and allow the dough to rise again for 30-35 minutes more, until doubled in volume.

Preheat an oven to 400 F, lightly grease a baking sheet. Deflate the dough and remove onto a work surface lightly dusted with flour, knead lightly. Place the dough on the prepared baking sheet and shape into an oval about 1/2-inch thick. Set aside to rise a third time for about 30 minutes. Bake in the preheated oven until nicely browned and hollow sounding when thumped, 20 to 25 minutes.

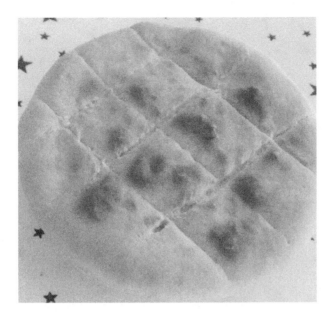

Kljukusa Pancakes

Preparation time: 10 minutes

Cooking time: 15 minutes

Ingredients

1 piece of onion

5 potatoes of a medium size

2 eggs

1 soup spoonful of flour

1 teaspoon of salt

1/2 teaspoon of dry rosemary

3 tablespoons of oil

Preparation

Grate the potatoes, chop the onion, add the eggs, salt, flour, oil and rosemary and mix. Pour the mass into an oiled baking mould by making "pancakes" of 4 inch in diameter. Bake them in the oven till they get yellow brownish. When they are all done, make "sandwiches" with cream, cheese, smoked meat and yogurt.

Buckwheat pie

Preparation time: 15 minutes
Cooking time: 60 minutes

Ingredients

Pancakes

2/3 pound of white wheat flour

2/3 pound of integral buckwheat flour

1 teaspoon of salt

2 tablespoons of oil

Water

Filling

2/3 pound of cottage cheese

2 eggs

1 cup of milk cream

1 cup of sour milk

1 cup of blanched finely chopped dock (nettle, spinach, chard)

Salt, pepper and basil

Preparation

Make the stuffing by mixing all the aforementioned ingredients well. Cheese should preserve its small balls. Add spices and make the mass for pancakes to be somewhat denser than the usual composition for pancakes. Put some oil in a round baking mould and start with layering. The first layer should be a pancake. Coat it with the filling and then place another pancake. Continue this process till you use up all the filling. The last layer of the pie should be the filling and pie could be cut prior or after baking. Bake at 360 F for about 25-30 minutes until the pie gets a yellow brownish color. Serve warm or cold with sour milk or yogurt.

Fish Pastry

Preparation time: 35 minutes
Cooking time: 40 minutes

Ingredients
1 pound (500 g) of white flour
1 cup (250 ml) of lukewarm water
1 tea spoon of salt
2/3 cup (1.5 dl) of oil
2 cup (500 ml) of sour milk or yogurt
5 cloves of finely chopped garlic

Preparation
Make the dough to be soft and not sticky to hands. Divide into 5 pieces and leave them for 30 minutes to rest, covered with a wet kitchen cloth. Use the rolling pin to flatten each dough piece like sheets for a pie. Sprinkle each dough sheet with oil and roll as you do for a pie. Place it in an oiled baking mould and repeat the procedure with the remaining dough pieces. Coat it all with oil once again. Cut the rolled pies in mouthful sized cubes. Bake in the oven at 390 F for 30 minutes or until it gets a yellow brownish color. Immediately after baking, pour the sour milk (spiced with garlic) on it. Serve warm.

Pihtije

Preparation time: 15 minutes
Cooking time: 190 minutes

Ingredients (5 servings)

4 pig trotters cut lengthwise into halves

1 smoked or raw pork hock

1 ox tail

2-3 bay leaves

A dozen of peppercorns

5 cloves of garlic

Salt to taste

Preparation

Place meat and 2 cloves of garlic into a large dish and add water, a few inches above the meat. Simmer for several hours on low heat in a covered dish, until meat falls apart completely and is separated from the bones. Remove cooked meat, separate from bones and skin, chop and return to the dish. Add chopped garlic and salt. Pour the mixture into small bowls and place into the refrigerator to cool and set at least for 12 hours. Remove the layer of fat from the surface and serve.

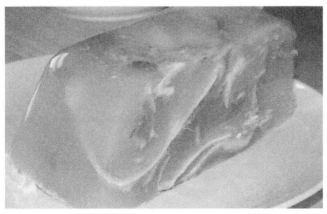

Domestic croissant (*Kiflice*)

Preparation time: 20 minutes
Cooking time: 45 minutes

Ingredients

1 pound of flour
1 pack of yeast
2 eggs
½ cup of milk
1/2 tablespoon of salt
2 tablespoons of oil
1 tablespoon of sugar

Preparation

Pour milk in a bowl with two spoons of sugar and a pack of yeast. Leave it and wait about 10 minutes for the yeast to rise up. Mix prepared flour, teaspoon of salt and an egg into another bowl.

When the yeast is risen up, pour the content of the first bowl into the other one and whisk them all well. Knead the dough until you get fine soft (not sticky) dough suitable for forming. On the table surface (or on a wide wooden plate) stretch dough with the wooden rolling pin to the thickness of about 1/5 inch, making a square form of the whole dough surface. Cut the stretched dough into smaller triangle pieces. The size of croissant depends on the baker, who rolls the sizes they want and like. Wrap each of the cut pieces diagonally from one angle to the opposite one, making nice dough rolls. Spread a thin layer of cooking oil over the baking pan surface and arrange the wrapped rolls into the baking pan, leaving some space between them as they tend to grow in size during the baking process. Separate one egg yolk in a small glass and whisk it well. Then, with a small brush, spread a thin layer of egg yolk over the upper surface of each roll. Sprinkle a little salt and sesame over each croissant.

Put the baking pan into the warmed up oven and bake the croissant at the temperature of 350°F for about half an hour. When the baking is finished pull out the pan from the oven and leave the croissants to cool off. Croissants can be filled with cheese, ham, pork or chicken pate during preparation.

Stretched pumpkin pie (*Tikvenik*)

Preparation time: 45 minutes
Cooking time: 45 minutes

Ingredients (5 servings)
1 pound of grated pumpkin
1 pound of flour
2 teaspoons of salt
1 ¼ cups of water

Preparation
Add flour and salt to the mixing bowl and immediately add prepared water. Knead the dough by hand until there are no lumps. Leave the dough to rest for 17 minutes. Dust the working surface with flour. Divide the dough into 2 equal parts and shape them into pie crusts. Each crust should be about half the thickness of human finger, in shape and size of the chosen baking pan. Grease the pan with a tablespoon of oil and add the first crust, grease its surface and add another crust. Let them rest for another 20 minutes. Start stretching them from the center and do not stick fingertips deep into the dough. Fill with the pumpkin filling. Bake at 360 F for about 40 minutes, until the crust has a nice golden color.

Cicvara

Preparation time: 15 minutes
Cooking time: 15 minutes

Ingredients (4 servings)
1 cup of water
1 cup of milk
2/3 pound of white cheese (or *kajmak*, see recipe in this cookbook)
8 tablespoons of corn flour
1 spoonful of solid lard
1 tablespoon of salt

Preparation
Add cheese and some water to a pan. Once the cheese has melted and water has boiled, add flour and further stir and cook. When *cicvara* is almost done, add butter or *kajmak*, cook for 3 more minutes and serve. In the rural areas butter or *kajmak* were added to a pan first, with a bit of water. Once it was cooked through, flour was added. Once everything was well done, cheese and milk were added, and everything was cooked until cheese had melted.

Vegan Gibanica

Preparation time: 25 minutes
Cooking time: 45 minutes

Ingredients (8 servings)
1 package of filo dough (defrosted)
½ cup of raw cashews (soaked for 4–6 hours or overnight)
1/4 teaspoon of garlic powder
1/4 teaspoon of onion powder
1 teaspoon of apple cider vinegar
1 tablespoon of nutritional yeast
2 tablespoons of cornstarch
1 pound of firm or medium tofu
2–3 tablespoons of olive oil for brushing
1–1 ½ teaspoons of sea salt
½ cup of water
1 cup of sparkling water
1 teaspoon of caraway seeds and more for sprinkling

Preparation
Preheat oven to 375°F. Generously grease a baking dish with olive oil and set aside. Process garlic powder, onion powder, soaked cashews, nutritional yeast, cornstarch, salt, vinegar and still water in a blender until smooth. In a large mixing bowl combine tofu and cashew mixture. Mash the tofu with a fork or potato masher. Taste for seasoning and add more salt if needed. Add caraway seeds and sparkling water and stir to combine. Unfold the filo dough and cover it with damp kitchen towel. Keep some water on the side to sprinkle over filo sheets. Do not let your filo dough dry out and get crumbly. Depending on the size of your baking dish, place 1 or 2 filo sheets on the bottom of it. Sprinkle with water and brush with a little bit of olive oil.

Take one filo sheet and crumple it as a piece of paper. Dip it into the tofu mixture, make sure it soaks up the liquid and the stuffing gets stuck inside. Place the ball inside the baking dish and repeat the process. Put the filo balls tightly next to each other until there's no more space. If some tofu mixture is left, spread it around, filling up holes. Cover with another filo sheet and tuck the sides in. Brush it generously with oil and sprinkle some caraway seeds and water on top. Bake for 40 minutes or until the top is golden brown and serve.

Levacha

Preparation time: 20 minutes
Cooking time: 55 minutes

Ingredients
2 eggs
1 cup of fine polenta
1 cup of self-rising flour
3 teaspoons of plain whole milk yogurt
1 cup of cottage cheese
4 teaspoons of olive oil
1 large grated zucchini
1 cup of water
1 cup of sour cream
Salt

Topping
2 eggs
4 heaped tablespoons of cottage cheese
4 heaped tablespoons of sour cream
4 tablespoons of olive oil
Salt to taste

Preparation
Preheat oven to 450 F. Beat eggs in a bowl and fold in oil. Sift in the polenta and self-rising flour and mix. Add water, grated zucchini, yogurt, cottage cheese and sour cream. Add salt to taste. It should have a batter-like consistency, but if too thick, add more water. Pour into a greased pan about 2–3 inches deep. Reduce oven temperature to 350 F and bake for up to 40 minutes. Remove from oven when cooked and using a knife slice the *levaca*

into diamond shapes while still in the pan. Mix all the topping ingredients and pour evenly over the baked base so that it soaks through. Return it to the oven for another 10 minutes. When ready take out of oven and leave to sit for 10 minutes before slicing and serving. Keep covered with a clean cotton or linen cloth.

Belmuz

Preparation time: 10 minutes

Cooking time: 35 minutes

Ingredients (4 servings)

1 ½ pounds of very fresh sheep cheese

1/3 pound of maize flour

Salt to taste

Preparation

Gently heat the cheese in a deep pot until it has melted but not boiled, then stir in the maize flour very gradually. Continue to cook while stirring continuously for up to 20 minutes. When the cheese comes together in a ball in the middle of the pot and the milk fat separates to the side, the *belmuz* is ready. Add salt to taste and serve hot with a variety of salads.

Chicken Aspic

Preparation time: 10 minutes
Cooking time: 80 minutes

Ingredients
1 pound of chicken breasts
6 ½ cups of water2 boiled eggs
1 barren of carrot
1 hot pepper
2/3 oz of gelatin
8 teaspoons of water
Salt and pepper
Parsley leaf

Preparation
Put the chicken breasts with bite and skin into a larger sherry, add spices and sprinkle with water. Cook at the moderate temperature for 55-65 minutes. Take the boiled meat out of the liquid and let it cool. Remove the skin and separate the flesh and bones, and shred the meat using a fork. Sort the reeds of cooked eggs at the bottom of a modular or another container, suitable for the preparation of salad bowl - silicone mold, etc. Decorate with parsley leaves, chopped peppers and carrots and then compare the prepared meat. Pour water over the gelatin and let it swell. In hot broth left from the meat, add the prepared gelatin and mix. Pour the gelatinous mass over the meat and place the bowl in the cold so that the aspic is tightened. Cover well-cooled mass with a large plate and leave for about 15 minutes. After that, gently lift the mold in order to slide the windscreen and completely fit the plate. Decorate according to taste and serve.

Baked cauliflower

Preparation time: 20 minutes
Cooking time: 35 minutes

Ingredients (5 servings)

1 piece of cauliflower

1 egg

1 tablespoon of flour

2 tablespoons of olive oil

1 cup of milk

1 garlic clove

1 tablespoon of wine vinegar

1 tablespoon of spice made from dried vegetables

Ground pepper to taste

Preparation

Clean cauliflower, separate into florets and wash. Boil in salted water, adding the wine vinegar. Fry the boiled cauliflower in hot oil with finely chopped garlic, pepper and salt. Transfer it to the baking pan. Whisk a tablespoon of dried vegetable spices, an egg, a cup of milk and a tablespoon of flour. Pour mixture over the cauliflower in the oven. When cauliflower gets brown, meal can be served.

Cauliflower steak

Preparation time: 35 minutes
Cooking time: 35 minutes

Ingredients (4 servings)
1 pound of cauliflower
2 eggs
1 onion
1/5 pound of ham
2 tablespoons of breadcrumbs
½ tablespoon of pepper
½ parsley
1/5 pound of cheese
2 tablespoons of milk

Preparation
Pour a little milk in boiling water and add the cauliflower. When tender, remove from water and leave it to cool. Mash the cauliflower and add finely chopped ham and onions, eggs, pepper and parsley. Combine everything and add 2 tablespoons of breadcrumbs. Make balls from the mixture. Cut prepared cheese into sticks and put them into cauliflower balls. Roll the balls in breadcrumbs and deep fry in oil until golden brown.

Ham and Egg Muffins

Preparation time: 22 minutes

Ingredients (for eight servings)

8 eggs

8 thin slices of deli-style cooked ham

1 ounce of mozzarella cheese or ¼ cup of shredded Italian cheese blend

8 teaspoons of basil pesto

8 halved cherry tomatoes or grape tomatoes

Ground black pepper

(Note: you will need muffin cups and nonstick cooking spray)

Preparation

Preheat the oven to 350 degrees F. Coat eight 2 1/2-inch muffin cups with cooking spray. Gently press a ham slice on the bottom and to the sides of each prepared muffin cup, carefully ruffling the edges of ham. Divide cheese among the ham-lined muffin cups. Break an egg into a measuring cup and transfer the egg into a muffin cup. Repeat with the remaining eggs. Sprinkle with pepper. Put 1 teaspoon of pesto on each egg (not mandatory). Top with tomato halves.

Bake for 19 minutes or until whites are completely set and yolks are thickened. Let sit in muffin cups for 3 to 5 minutes before serving.

Lasagna Burek

Preparation time: 20 minutes
Cooking time: 150 minutes

Ingredients (4 servings)

Dough
2 ¼ pounds of soft flour
2 tablespoons of oil
2 teaspoons of salt
1 1/2 cups of lukewarm water

Filling
½ pound of mushrooms
1 pound of cheddar or any similar cheese
1 pound of minced beef or pork meat
2 cups of thick tomato juice
2 teaspoons of oregano
1 tablespoon of sugar
1/2 teaspoon of salt
1/4 teaspoon of black pepper
2 tablespoons of oil

Oiling
1/2 packages of margarine
1 cup of oil

Preparation

Make the dough by combining oil, salt and flour, then slowly add lukewarm water and work it into soft, compact dough that doesn't stick. Divide it into 6 balls, oil them and cover with a plastic bag. Leave it for 70 minutes to rest then flatten the balls into discs of about 8 inch in diameter and leave them to rest for 35-40 minutes.

Filling

Heat 2 tablespoons of oil, add the minced meat and fry it until the water reduces, add the spices, tomato juice and sugar and cook for 16 minutes, until it reduces a bit. If not thick enough, add a dash of flour. Leave the sauce to cool down as it must not be warm at all. Also prepare the chopped mushrooms and the grated cheese.

Preheat the oven to 420 F. Take a large tablecloth and sprinkle flour on it. Take the first dough disc, put it on the tablecloth and start pulling gently on the ends to stretch it paper thin. If dough is not extremely stretchy, wait another minute and continue. Spread into a circle of 5 ft in diameter. Take the melted margarine and oil and apply gently all over the dough with a brush. Tear away any thick edges of the dough and fold it like an envelope into a rectangular shape, oiling every fold, so that the folded edges intertwine. Put it aside. Stretch another dough disc, oil it and put the former rectangle in the center. On the rectangle apply 1/4 of the sauce, mushrooms and cheese and fold the thin dough around it like an envelope again, oiling every folded side. Put the whole thing aside and repeat this step one more time. Do the same with the remaining ingredients. Put on baking paper and into preheated oven, bake until golden brown and crunchy.

Mantije

Preparation time: 60 minutes
Baking time: 40 minutes

Ingredients (5 servings)
2 1/5 pounds of fresh young white cheese
5 eggs
1/3 pound of melted butter
1 pound of flour
2 tablespoons of salt
3 ½ tablespoons of oil
1 cup of lukewarm water
Salt

Preparation
Mash the cheese, adding salt and beaten eggs. Mix well. Prepare smooth dough from it and divide it into four dough balls. Brush each ball with oil and leave to rest for 45 minutes. Roll the sheets as thin as possible and place the prepared cheese filling along one edge. Slowly roll the dough in a cylinder. Cut the dough into squares, close the ends and place them in a greased pan. Top with melted butter. Bake at 480 F for 30 minutes. While hot, the dish should be topped with sour cream and baked for additional 5 minutes.

Soups

Domestic Broth (*Domaca chorba*)

Preparation time: 15 minutes
Cooking time: 45 minutes

Ingredients (5 servings)

3 tablespoons of oil

2/3 pound of veal

2/3 cup of rice

1 medium onion

2 carrots

1 cup of chopped mixed root vegetables

Salt, pepper, parsley leaf to taste

Preparation

Fry finely chopped meat and vegetables in hot oil for a short period of time. Add about 12 cups of water and cook on medium heat for about 20 minutes. Add seasonings according to taste. Add more water if needed and cook for 15-20 minutes.

Spinach soup

Preparation time: 15 minutes
Cooking time: 50 minutes

Ingredients (4 servings)

1 pound of spinach (or orache)
4 tablespoons of flour
2 tablespoons of lard
1 paprika
1 egg
Wine vinegar

Preparation

Rinse spinach well, chop and add to 2 cups of water. Bring water to a boil and then discard the water. Add a new volume of water and cool for about 20 minutes. Fry flour with molten lard, add some paprika and fry them together shortly. Pour the roux into the soup, and then add a beaten egg, in order to make irregular bits. Cook for another 15 minutes and add vinegar to taste.

Nettle Pottage

Preparation time: 15 minutes
Cooking time: 30 minutes

Ingredients

1 onion
1/3 pound of beech forest mushrooms
½ pound of grated pumpkin
1/3 pound of nettle leaves
2 cloves of garlic
Salt and pepper
2 tablespoons of oil
4 ¼ cups of water

Preparation

Fry the finely chopped onion, garlic and grated pumpkin in oil in a pan of adequate size. When the pumpkin gets soft, add the finely chopped mushrooms and nettle. Add the water and spices. and cook for another 5 minutes, after boiling.

Classic Vegetable Soup

Preparation time: 10 minutes
Cooking time: 60 minutes

Ingredients (7 servings)
1/2 cup of dry and slightly salty cheese
3 large onions, peeled and chopped
3 carrots, peeled and cut into large pieces
1/2 pound of spinach, washed, trimmed, and shredded
1/4-inch slices
2 celery ribs, trimmed and cut
2 large potatoes, peeled and diced
4 large ripe tomatoes, peeled and chopped
1 finely chopped bunch of parsley
8 cups of water
1 cup of olive oil
Salt
Freshly ground black pepper
Juice of 1/2-1 lemon

Preparation

In a large soup pot, heat half the olive oil and add onions. Cook while stirring over medium heat until wilted, 6-8 minutes. Add the celery and carrots and toss to coat with oil. Sauté in the pot for 5 minutes, stirring. Add the potatoes and stir to coat. Add the parsley and the tomatoes. Pour in the water, season with salt, and bring the soup to a boil.

Reduce the heat and simmer for 30 minutes. Add the spinach and simmer another 20 minutes. Adjust the seasoning with salt, pepper, and lemon juice.

Pour in the remaining raw olive oil just before serving. Ladle into individual bowls and sprinkle a few teaspoons of the grated cheese on top.

Chicken and Eggplant Soup

Preparation time: 15 minutes
Cooking time: 60 minutes

Ingredients (8 servings)

6 cups of peeled, diced (1-inch) eggplants

¼ cup of extra-virgin olive oil plus

1 tablespoon of extra-virgin olive oil plus

1 ½ teaspoons of divided salt

¼ teaspoon of ground pepper

1 cup of chopped onions

2 tablespoons of chopped garlic

1 medium red bell pepper, diced

2 tablespoons of sweet Hungarian paprika

2 teaspoons of hot Hungarian paprika

¼ cup of chopped fresh parsley

1 ½ tablespoons of chopped fresh oregano

1 teaspoon of ground turmeric

½ teaspoon of ground ginger

7 cups of low-sodium chicken broth or stock

1 pound of boneless, skinless chicken breast (trimmed and cut into 1-inch pieces)

1 cup of half-and-half milk

2 large egg yolks

1 ½ tablespoons of cornstarch

¼ cup of freshly squeezed lemon juice

Lemon wedges for serving

Preparation

Preheat oven to 400 degrees F. Toss eggplant in a medium bowl with 1/4 cup oil, 1/2 teaspoon, salt and pepper. Spread in a single layer on a large rimmed baking sheet. Roast for 10 minutes and turn the eggplant over and roast until very soft, for another 10 minutes. Meanwhile, heat the remaining 1 tablespoon oil in a large pot over medium heat. Add onion and garlic, cover and cook. Stir occasionally, until the onion is soft, up to 10 minutes. Stir in bell pepper and cook, uncovered, for another 2 minutes. Sprinkle sweet and hot paprika (or cayenne to taste) over the vegetables and stir until well coated. Stir in the oregano, eggplant, parsley, turmeric and ginger until well mixed. Add broth and chicken and ring to a boil over high heat. Reduce the heat and simmer for 10 minutes and whisk egg yolks, half-and-half and cornstarch in a medium bowl. Stir in 1 cup of the hot broth until combined. Gradually stir this mixture back into the pot, taking care that it does not boil, which will scramble the eggs. Whisk in lemon juice and season with the remaining 1 teaspoon salt. Serve with lemon wedges, if desired.

Sour Chicken Soup

Preparation time: 120 minutes
Cooking time: 35 minutes

Ingredients (8 servings)
1 finely chopped large carrot
1 finely chopped large potato
½ cup of pouring cream
1 egg yolk
½ a lemon juice
Chopped flat-leaf parsley

Chicken stock
½ bunch of flat-leaf parsley
½ bunch of thyme
2 roughly chopped carrots
1 roughly chopped tomato
1 peeled, roughly chopped swede
5 roughly chopped, trimmed celery stalks
1 trimmed chopped leek (white part only)
1 trimmed, skin on, halved onion
3 ¼ pounds of chicken wings
1 chicken carcass
3 bay leaves
2 tablespoons of black peppercorns

Preparation
Tie the thyme and parsley together with kitchen string and place in a large saucepan with vegetables, onion, chicken carcass, chicken wings and bay leaves, and cover with 10 cups of water. Bring to the boil, then skim scum from

surface, add peppercorns and reduce heat to low–medium. Cover partially and simmer for 140-150 minutes. Strain through a fine sieve into a large bowl and discard all solids except chicken wings. Cool slightly, then refrigerate stock and chicken wings overnight. Skim fat from stock and transfer to a large saucepan. Bring to a boil, then add carrots and potatoes, and simmer for 7-9 minutes or until vegetables are tender. Meanwhile, discard the skin and bones from the chicken wings and reserve 1 cup of meat. Refrigerate remaining meat for another use. Add reserved chicken to soup and simmer until heated through. Remove from heat. Combine cream and egg yolk in a bowl, then stir into soup with lemon juice. Season with salt and pepper.

Tomato soup with white cheese topping

Preparation time: 15 minutes
Cooking time: 20 minutes

Ingredients (4 servings)

1 onion
2 cloves of garlic
4 tomatoes
1 3/4 can of crushed tomatoes
2 tablespoons of tomato puree
1/2 bunch of fresh basil
1/3 bunch of oregano
1 teaspoon of salt
1 teaspoon of black pepper
1/3 pint of vegetable stock
2 tablespoons of white wine
3 tablespoons of *ajvar* (optional)
1 teaspoon of sambal oelek (optional)
1 can of crème fraiche
1/2 box of white cheese (or feta)

Preparation

Chop the onion and let it sizzle in a pot with butter or olive oil. Chop the tomatoes and garlic, add them to the onion and let them sizzle. Pour the crushed tomatoes in the pot. Season with herbs, add the stock and let it boil for 5 minutes. Mix the crème fraiche and white cheese with a fork. Put it in the fridge. Mix the soup with a rod mixer and put it on the stove again. Let it simmer for another 5-6 minutes. Put the cream in your bowl of soup and add basil or oregano to taste.

Ajnpren broth

Preparation time: 10 minutes
Cooking time: 25 minutes

Ingredients (5 servings)
6 tablespoons of flour
1 tablespoon of lard or butter
1 tablespoon of paprika
Cups of water
2 eggs
Salt, pepper and parsley leaf

Preparation
Heat the lard and add 2 tablespoons of flour and fry for a short time. Stir constantly and add paprika. Whisk eggs and 4 tablespoons of flour and gradually add water. Once the broth is boiling, add the batter in a thin trickle. Add seasonings according to taste and cook for 4-5 minutes. Add sour cream to taste when serving.

White Soup with Garlic and Lemon

Preparation time: 15 minutes
Cooking Time: 110 minutes

Ingredients (2 servings)

8.8 oz of cannellini beans or small white beans soaked in water overnight

6 tablespoons of extra virgin olive oil

1 carrot, cut into very thin slices

1 finely chopped stick of celery

½ minced onion

3 chopped garlic cloves

1 lemon zest and juice

Salt and freshly ground pepper

Preparation

Beans

Drain the beans from the water they've been soaking in overnight. Fill a cooking pot with water halfway and add the beans. Bring to a boil over high heat. Cook for 4 minutes and drain the beans in a strainer.

Soup

In a medium-sized cooking pot, add the olive oil and heat over medium-high heat. Add the onion and garlic and cook until softened and golden in color. Add the beans, along with 6 cups of water (part of it could be vegetable stock), and bring to a boil. Then reduce the heat to medium-low; and with the lid partially open on the side, simmer for about 120 minutes or until beans are completely soft and tender. Cooking time depends specifically on the variety and quality of the beans.

Add the celery and carrot and season with salt and pepper. Continue simmering, stirring occasionally until the soup gets nice and thick. Then add the lemon juice and zest and cook for 3 more minutes. Remove from the heat and serve with freshly ground pepper on top and an extra squeeze of fresh lemon to taste.

Lunch and dinner

Musaka

Musaka is a traditional dish in several Balkan countries. The Greek version of musaka (*Moussaka*) is made with eggplant while many other regions use potatoes. They are sliced and layered with ground beef or pork, then covered in a yogurt egg sauce before baking. It is very easy to assemble and makes quite a bit; plenty of leftovers for a family of four. The musaka can be assembled up to two days ahead of baking time. Just add the yogurt sauce right before it goes in the oven. If you add the sauce earlier, it may separate a bit, and won't look as good.

Preparation Time: 30 minutes
Cooking Time: 75 minutes

Ingredients
1/4 cup (60 ml) of olive oil
4 pounds (1,8 kg) of russet potatoes
1 medium onion, chopped
1 pound (450 gr) of ground beef or pork
Salt and pepper to taste

Topping
4 eggs
1 cup (240 ml) of yogurt or sour cream
2 cups (480 ml) of milk
Salt and pepper to taste

Preparation
Peel the russet potatoes and slice into 1/4 inch (no larger) thick circles. In a large pan, heat a drizzle of olive oil over medium heat. Add onions and cook, stirring often, until lightly browned. Stir in ground meat, breaking up with a

spoon, and season with salt and pepper. Continue cooking and breaking the meat apart until browned.

Preheat oven to 400 °F (200°C) and grease a 9x13 inch baking dish with olive oil. Layer half of the sliced potatoes, about two layers, on the bottom of the prepared baking dish. Season with salt and pepper. Cover with the cooked ground meat. Layer the remaining potatoes, another two layers.

In a medium bowl, whisk together the eggs, yogurt, milk, salt and pepper. Pour evenly over the potatoes until it is right below the top layer. Bake in the preheated oven until potatoes are tender and top is golden brown, about one hour. Broil, if desired, to crisp the top further.

Wait 15 minutes before slicing and serving.

Stuffed cabbage rolls (*Sarma*)

Sarma, translated as *"a stuffed thing,"* is made and enjoyed at homes and in restaurants during the winter months in the Balkans. However, many Eastern European nations call the same dish different names. From *holubky* in Czech Republic and Slovakia, to *golabki* in Poland and *lahana, dolmasi* in Turkey – *sarma* is everywhere. These stuffed cabbage dumplings are traditionally filled with rice, parsley and ground meat, which we substitute with mushrooms, and simmer in a broth of tomato paste, bay leaf, and paprika. Serve *sarma* as a main dish, with a side of potatoes to soak up the juice from the stew.

Preparation Time: 15 minutes
Cooking Time: 180 minutes

Ingredients

2 medium sized pieces of sour cabbage (20-25 good leaves)
1 3/4 pounds (780 g) of mixed minced meat (more beef, less pork)
A smaller piece of smoked bacon
Some smoked pork ribs
6 onions
1 cup (230gr) of rice
3 dried red peppers
1 tablespoon of flour
1 cup (240 ml) of oil
Salt
Pepper
Dried vegetable seasoning
Laurel leaf
Ground red pepper

Preparation

Taste sourness of the sour cabbage, separate the leaves, and if it is necessary, pour water over it to reduce acidity and saltiness. While cabbage is in the water, fry finely chopped onions in half of the oil, then add the mixed minced meat and fry it as well. Add salt and pepper, and sprinkle with ground red pepper and dried vegetable seasoning. Add rice. Mix everything together and remove from stove.

Clean cabbage leaves from thickenings by patting them dry between 2 paper towels after they've been in the water, but carefully not to tear the cabbage leaves. On each leaf, put some of the filling of fried meat and onions, and roll the cabbage rolls (*sarma* is one roll), first from yourself, then from the sides, then again from yourself and place them in a suitable cooking pot. It is best to fit the cabbage rolls in one layer, but not too tight against one another. Between cabbage rolls, put in a few pieces of smoked bacon cut pieces and smoked pork ribs. Crush the laurel leaf and dried red peppers and sprinkle over the cabbage rolls.

Pour water over all, so the cabbage rolls are covered. In the beginning, cook on a high temperature (until the water boils), and then at a medium temperature for 20 minutes.

Using the other half of the oil, fry the flour, add a little ground pepper, whisk, and pour all over cabbage rolls while they are cooking. Shake the pan so the browned flour spreads evenly throughout and separate the cabbage rolls with a spoon just a little so the water and browned flour can coalesce with each other into a complete sauce.

Place the dish in the pre-heated oven and bake on a medium temperature for about 2 hours. The temperature should not exceed 392°F (200°C). If cabbage rolls start to become brown on the surface, cover them with foil, but do not seal them, so that the steam is still able to evaporate. If, during the time of cooking, all the water evaporates, add a little hot water. Cabbage needs to be cooked for long and thoroughly. Remove the cooked cabbage rolls from the oven and serve with the pieces of smoked bacon and pork ribs.

Green rolls (Sarmica od zelja)

This type of *sarma* also originates from Turkey, however it is common in many other countries that were under the Ottoman Empire. The name itself means "wrapping" in Turkish, but in this case, mothers often add the prefix *"green."* For this type of *sarma*, our mothers use collard greens, chard, or grape leaves. They are eaten with yogurt and bread.

Preparation Time: 30 minutes
Cooking Time: 120 minutes

Ingredients

1 large red onion, finely chopped
1 pound (450 gr) of ground beef
2 cups (460 gr) of washed rice
1 carrot, shredded
20 collard green leaves
Salt and pepper
2 tablespoons of flour
1 tablespoon of paprika
4 tablespoons of oil
Water
Yogurt

Preparation

Stew chopped onions for 15 minutes in a little bit of water, add ground beef, rice and oil. Add salt and pepper to taste. If needed, add more water, as the rice will absorb most of it. Add shredded carrot and continue to stew for another 20-25 minutes (total time should be about 40-45 minutes).

While the filling is being stewed, wash collard greens. Boil water in a large pot and remove from heat. Place leaves into the hot water and allow to soak for 45 minutes. Then take the leaves out of the water and use the stewed filling to make *sarma* rolls. Save this water for later use. Place rolls vertically in a pot and make sure you fill the whole pot, so they don't fall over and unwrap. Use the leftover water from the steaming of the leaves to almost cover the *sarma* rolls in the pot.

Slow cook *sarmas* on low heat for 3 hours. When the *sarmas* are done cooking, brown some flour in oil and add a teaspoon of paprika. Add all over the top.

Beans (Pasulj)

Again, there are a million versions of this unique and popular dish, but meat is always a part of pasulj - ideally smoked meat. This can be smoked bacon or a good smoked sausage. In this version of the recipe, you will use both, the sausage being a well smoked kielbasa.

Preparation Time: 15 minutes
Cooking Time: 180 minutes

Ingredients

1 pound (450 gr) of canned white beans or 1 pound (450 gr) of dried white beans (navy beans or cannellini)
2 tablespoons of olive or sunflower oil
1/4 pound (120 gr) of smoked streaky bacon
1 large onion, chopped
2 cloves of garlic, chopped
1 bell pepper, red or green: cored, seeded and chopped
3 bay leaves
1 tablespoon of chopped parsley
6 whole peppercorns
2 heaping teaspoons of sweet paprika
1 heaping teaspoon of hot paprika
3 tablespoons of tomato paste
1 pound (450 gr) of kielbasa or other smoked simmering sausage, thickly sliced
1/2 teaspoon of salt

Preparation

Put the beans in a colander and pick them over to get rid of any grit or discolored beans. Rinse them a couple of times in cold water. Then put the beans in a large saucepan, cover them about an inch or two in water, and bring them to a boil. Lower the heat to a simmer and let the beans cook gently for half an hour. At the end of that time, remove the pot from the heat and pour a liter or so of cold water over the beans to stop the cooking. Allow them to rest for ten minutes or so, then drain the water off and set them aside.

Dry the big pot and add olive oil or sunflower oil. Add the chopped bacon and sauté it gently until it starts to brown and its fat runs. Then add the chopped onions and fry until translucent. Add the chopped garlic, bay leaves, chopped parsley and peppercorns. (Make sure you do not add the salt at this point. If you add it now, the beans will refuse to get tender when you cook them.) Finally, add the paprika, frying everything gently for about five minutes thereafter.

Add about a liter of boiling water and the beans. Stir well, and add the tomato paste, cover.
Turn the heat down and allow the soup to simmer very gently for at least 1 1/2 to 2 hours, until the beans are soft. (You will need to keep checking the beans for their degree of doneness: they may take as long as three hours' simmering to become soft, depending on the particular batch of beans.) About an hour before the soup is ready, add the kielbasa.
A little before serving time, check the taste, and then add the salt. Do it a little at a time, so as not to over salt.

Finally, before serving, use a potato masher or a broad spoon to mash some of the cooked beans against the side of the pot so they somewhat thicken the soup.

Djuvech (*Ɖuveč*)

Djuvech (Đuveč) is a very popular casserole in the Balkans that features a variety of vegetables and your choice of meat. The most famous one is from Bosnia and Herzegovina. The biggest advantage of this dish is that you can easily omit the meat for a vegetarian dish.

Preparation Time: 15 minutes
Cooking Time: 130 minutes

Ingredients

½ cup (120 ml) of oil
2 pounds (900gr) of meat, cut into bite sized pieces, can use chicken or beef
1½ pounds (680gr) of onion
3¼ pounds (1,5 kg) of tomatoes
1 medium sized eggplant
1 green pepper
2 zucchinis
2 celery stalks, sliced
2 cups (480 ml) of water
½ cup (120 ml) of vegetable oil
1 cup (230 gr) of rice
Parsley
Salt and pepper, to taste

Preparation

Slice the tomatoes. Chop the onions into about 1/4" pieces. Peel and cut the eggplant, green pepper and zucchini into medium sized pieces. Mix the onions, eggplant, green pepper, zucchini and celery in a large bowl with the oil. Salt and pepper to taste. Take a casserole dish and layer the ingredients in the following order: First, place half of the sliced tomatoes. Top with half of the vegetable mixture. Add the meat. Then add the other half of the vegetables, the uncooked rice, and top with the remaining tomato slices. Pour the water over the casserole. Cover and bake in a 350°F (180°C) oven for 2 hours. Serve from the dish in which you prepared the *djuvech*.

Yellow Bean Soup (*Boranija*)

There are four ways to prepare *boranija*. No guys, this is not a soup, this is a main dish. Again, originally with meat (mainly with chicken), but it could be vegetarian too!

Preparation Time: 15 minutes
Cooking Time: 100 minutes

Ingredients
2 pounds (900 gr) of yellow wax beans
2 small onions
4 cloves of garlic
2 tablespoons of butter
1 1/2 tablespoons of all-purpose flour
10-12 tablespoons of chicken granules
1 tablespoon of paprika
Salt and black pepper
Crushed red pepper flakes
4 eggs
1 tablespoon of vinegar

Preparation
Clean, trim, and cut the beans into bite-size pieces. Chop the onions and mince the garlic. Melt the butter in a large Dutch oven or a heavy-bottomed pot. Add the onions and garlic, as well as a pinch of salt, and sauté until translucent. Add the flour and paprika and stir until the flour is dissolved and the onion mixture is thickened. Add the beans and enough water to cover (approximately 6 cups). Bring to a boil and add 6 more cups of water. Stir in the chicken granules (adjust amount to your preference), black pepper and red

pepper flakes to taste. Return to a boil, then reduce to a simmer. Simmer for 2 1/2 hours, covered.

Beat the eggs in a small bowl or a measuring cup. Turn off the heat and hold a fork over the soup. Pour the beaten eggs through the tines of the fork into the soup. Add one tablespoon of distilled vinegar, stir, and serve with a dollop of sour cream.

Peas stew with beef/lumb (*Grašak sa mesom*)

This is a typical Balkan dish, very popular in Serbia. It's a hearty meal, so it's good for wintertime, as it keeps you warm. Usually, it's served with traditional vermicelli rice.

Preparation Time: 15 minutes
Cooking Time: 80 minutes

Ingredients

1 ½ pounds (680 gr) of boneless lamb
½ pound (230 gr) of onions
1 pound (450 gr) of fresh green peas
½ pound (230 gr) of potatoes
1 tablespoon of lard (or 2 tablespoons of oil)
2 teaspoons of red dried paprika
1/2 teaspoon of dried thyme
1 cup (240 ml) of white dry wine
3 cups (720 ml) of water
1 teaspoon of salt
1/2 teaspoon of pepper

Preparation

Cut meat into large pieces, 1 inch (2,5 cm). Finely mince onions and put it into a pot with lard. Sauté onions until they become soft and transparent. Add meat and sauté until meat starts to release liquid. Add paprika, thyme, salt and pepper and stir.

Add wine and sauté until the alcohol evaporates. Add some water and cook for about 30 minutes.

In the meantime, peel the potatoes and cut them into small cubes (½ inch or 1,2 cm). Remove green peas from shuck. Add green peas and potatoes into stew and cook until all ingredients become soft and the liquid is reduced a bit.

Meatballs (Ćufte)

Meatballs are popular everywhere, from Turkey to Sweden. However, if you want meatballs that are authentically Balkan, you should prepare them in tomato sauce and serve with mashed potatoes.

Preparation Time: 30 minutes
Cooking Time: 60 minutes

Ingredients
1 1/3 pounds (600gr) of mixed minced meat
1 slice of bread soaked in milk
1 bunch of parsley
2 onions
1 egg
2 tablespoons of flour
4 tablespoons of oil
2 cups (480 ml) of tomato juice
Little sugar
1 teaspoon of ground red pepper
Salt
Pepper

Preparation
Clean onions, wash, cut, and whisk well in a wooden mortar. You can also chop onions in small pieces and then fry in a little oil, but the first method is better. Soak bread in milk and leave it to swell.

Blend together the onions with the meat, add squeezed soaked bread, and salt. Sprinkle the dried vegetables, spices, pepper, finely chopped parsley leaf and the egg, and mix well. Leave mixture to sit twenty minutes (if you have time, can sit more) in a cool place. Moisten your hands and make meatballs. Roll them in flour and fry in hot oil until golden brown on both sides.

In the hot oil, fry 2 tablespoons of flour. Add a little ground pepper, pour tomatoes, add salt and a little sugar on the top of a kitchen knife and stir the sauce until thick. When the sauce is finished, drop the meatballs in it, and let the dish simmer slowly for 1-2 minutes, stirring. Serve the meatballs in sauce.

Balkan Baked Sauerkraut (*Podvarak*)

This is a Balkan dish made from finely chopped sauerkraut, onions and meat (usually pork roast or chicken), which are combined and baked in an oven. Another description of *podvarak* is "*roast meat en sauerkraut.*" *Podvarak* can also be baked with a variety of other vegetables and additional meats. Sauerkraut, directly translated, means "sour cabbage." It is finely shredded cabbage that has been fermented by various lactic acid bacteria, including *Leuconostoc, Lactobacillus,* and *Pediococcus.*

Preparation Time: 20 minutes
Cooking Time: 120 minutes

Ingredients
1½ pounds (680 gr) of sauerkraut
Three-pound fried cut up and salted chicken
7 tablespoons of bacon fat or lard
½ cup (120 ml) of finely chopped onions
¼ teaspoon of finely chopped garlic
1 tablespoon of finely chopped hot chili peppers
Freshly ground black pepper
½ cup (120 ml) of chicken stock

Preparation
Wash the sauerkraut under cold running water, and then soak it in cold water for 10 to 20 minutes to reduce its sourness. Squeeze it dry by hand. Wash the chicken pieces quickly under cold running water, pat them dry with paper towels and salt generously. Over high heat, in a heavy 10-inch skillet, heat 4 tablespoons of fat until a light haze forms over it.

Brown the chicken pieces a few at a time, starting with the skin side down and turning them with tongs. As each piece browns, remove to a platter and add a fresh piece to the pan until all the chicken is done. Set aside. Heat the rest of the fat in the skillet until a light haze forms over it and add the onions and garlic. Cook for 2-3 minutes, or until the onions are slightly translucent.

Add the sauerkraut, chili peppers and a few grindings of black pepper. Cook uncovered for 10 minutes over medium heat. Using the tongs, lay the chicken pieces on top of the sauerkraut, and pour the stock over the chicken. Bring the liquid to a boil, then reduce the heat to low and cook, covered, for 30 minutes, or until the chicken is tender. Serve the sauerkraut on a platter with the chicken, either surrounding it or as a bed for it.

Stuffed Peppers (*Punjene Paprike*)

A traditional Serbian recipe for a classic dish of peppers stuffed with meat and vegetables. Again, there are many variations of stuffed peppers across the Balkans, but here is the basic recipe that you can modify by taste.

Preparation Time: 30 minutes
Cooking Time: 60 minutes

Ingredients

8 red peppers
1 pound (450 gr) of beef/pork minced meat combo
½ cup (120 gr) of rice
1 big sliced carrot
2 chopped onions
1 egg
1 tablespoon of chopped parsley, salt or *Vegeta* (local mixed spice available around the globe)
1 potato or tomato to close paprika
1 cup (240 ml) of tomato paste or tomato juice
10 tablespoons of oil
2 tablespoons of plain flour
1 tablespoon of ground red paprika (hot if wanted)

Preparation

Fry finely chopped onions and sliced carrots in 5 tablespoons of oil. After a few minutes, add minced meat. Add salt, *Vegeta* to taste and continue to fry for another 5 minutes, pressing the meat with your spoon to make the pieces smaller.

Take it off the heat and add rice and an egg. Stir the mixture and spoon the mixture into the peppers for 2/3 of its height. Cover the top of each paprika with a slice of a potato or a tomato, depending on what you prefer. Place peppers in a big pot or a deep pan.

In a saucepan, heat 5 tablespoons of oil and add 2 tablespoons of flour. Stir it for about 3 minutes. Quickly stir in the minced garlic and ground red paprika. Mix to a thin paste. Add the saucepan mixture, tomato juice or paste to paprika peppers and cover them with water. Add a little bit of *Vegeta* if desired and sprinkle chopped parsley on top.

Put the pot into the oven and leave it for 1 hour on 475°F (250°C). You can also choose to boil it at a lower temperature for 40-45 minutes.

Home Cooked Fresh Cabbage (*Slatki kupus*)

Yet another cabbage meal, and you will love it, for sure. A vegetarian version is also possible. In this region, we label this dish as a "*sweet cabbage*," but don't worry, it is not actually sweet.

Preparation Time: 20 minutes
Cooking Time: 60 minutes

Ingredients

1 medium sized cabbage
1 medium sized onion
¼ cup (60 gr) of rice
1 tablespoon and 1 teaspoon of ground red pepper
1 tablespoon and 2 teaspoons of a condiment (dry seasoned vegetables or *Vegeta* spice)
1 pound (450 gr) of pig rump meat, cut into small cubes
1 pound (450 gr) of smoked pork ribs
5-6 pieces of bacon (dry or smoked, according to taste)
¾ cup (180 ml) of cooked tomatoes (or 2 fresh tomatoes)
1 tablespoon of vinegar
5 tablespoons of cooking oil
1 tablespoon of flour
2 cups (960 ml) of water

Preparation

Place and arrange one half of the sliced cabbage onto the bottom of a 6 cups (1,4 kg) capacity cooking pan. Over the sliced cabbage, place a chopped medium sized onion and pour 50 gr of rice over the onion. Add 1 teaspoon of ground red pepper and 2 teaspoons of dry seasoned vegetables or *Vegeta*. Place and arrange 1 pound (450 gr) of pig rump meat, cut into small pieces (cubes), over it. Place and arrange 1 pound (450 gr) of smoked ribs over the pig rump meat and 5-6 pieces of bacon over the top of the meat. Arrange the other half of the sliced cabbage on top of these layers. Add ¾ cup of cooked tomatoes and 1 tablespoon of dry seasoned vegetables or *Vegeta*.

Pour 2 cups (960 ml) of water into the pan. Turn on the stove and cook the mixture in the pan for about 1 hour, keeping the temperature at about 400°F (200°C). This is the approximate time for meat to be cooked. During this time, all the other ingredients will be cooked, too.

At around halfway through the cooking time, add 1 tablespoon of vinegar and keep cooking. Stir the cooking contents from time to time. About 10-15 minutes before the end of cooking, lower the temperature to a simmer.

Take a small saucepan, pour in 5 tablespoons of cooking oil, add 1 tablespoon of flour, fry it for a few minutes, then add 1 tablespoon of ground red pepper. Stir it well, fry it briefly and pour this content into the main cooking pan with the cooking cabbage.

Keep cooking for about 10 more minutes. Turn off the stove, leaving the cooking pan on, while the plate is still hot. Prepare and arrange the dining table. Serve this warm, home cooked fresh cabbage as a main meal without any sides or salad, except bread, and enjoy this extraordinary taste.

Karadjordjeva steak (Karadjordjeva šnicla)

This dish is locally known as "a girl's dream." Very popular, but there are only a couple of ways to make a good Karadjordjeva steak.

Preparation Time: 10 minutes
Cooking Time: 20 minutes

Ingredients
1 ¾ pounds (780 gr) of pork or veal fillet
¼ pound (120 gr) of seasoned *kajmak*
1 oz (30 gr) of flour
1 egg
1 oz (30 gr) of bread crumbs
Oil
Salt

Preparation
Slice the fillet so that you get a sizeable steak. Pound the meat until it is thin and soft on both sides. Make one edge of the steak thinner so that it sticks easily once the meat is rolled up. Spread *kajmak* along the thicker edge and roll the meat into a cylinder shape. Coat the stuffed meat with flour and remove the excess flour. First, dip it into the beaten egg on all sides and then in the bread crumbs. Roll the meat on a clean surface so that the bread crumbs stick better. Fry in hot oil until golden yellow.

Chiken/pork and bell pepper stew (Pileći ili svinjski paprikaš)

Preparation Time: 20 minutes
Cooking Time: 90 minutes

Ingredients

1 Chicken, chopped into pieces
2 pounds (900 gr) of Red Desiree potatoes
3 large onions
2 carrots
1 bell pepper
2 tablespoons of paprika
1 tablespoon of tomato paste
2 Bay leaves
Salt
Vegeta

Preparation

Sauté the onions with 2 tablespoons of oil. Add the chopped carrots and bell peppers and continue to fry for another 5 minutes. Add chicken pieces and simmer for about 17 minutes, covered. Sprinkle with paprika, tomato paste, bay leaves, and add some water just enough to cover meat and cook further until cooked through. If water evaporates, continue to add some more to keep the meat covered. Cook on low heat. When the meat is half cooked, add potatoes and more water to make it like a stew. Continue to cook until the potatoes are ready. Then add salt, *Vegeta*, and pepper to taste, adding some parsley leaves if you like. Serve with fresh garden salad and crusty bread.

Serbian baked beans (*Prebranac*)

Of course, this dish is not only Serbian, since so many varieties under different names exist around the region. *Prebranac* is rich, comforting, and tasty. This baked bean dish is like a warm hug from the Balkans, the "Heart of Europe." The key is to slowly cook the onion until the golden sweetness develops.

Preparation Time: 10 minutes
Cooking Time: 120 minutes

Ingredients
1 pound (450 gr) of beans
1 ½ cups (350 ml) of oil
2 pounds (900 gr) of onions and 2 cloves of garlic
1 bay leaf
Paprika powder
Ground pepper and salt

Preparation
Put white beans in a pot, cover them with water, and bring to a boil. Drain, pour hot water over them, and cook until the beans are soft. Then drain them again. Peel an onion and put it to rest in cold water for about ten minutes. Then slice it into thin rounds. Heat one part of the oil and fry the onions until they turn golden. Add a bit of ground pepper, paprika powder and salt.

Cover the bottom of the dish with oil and then spread the beans evenly. Pour the fried onions over them. Then add the beans and the onions again until you run out of them. Always pour some oil on the layer of onions. The last layer has to be of beans. Put a bay leaf on top as well as two cloves of garlic and a dry, hot pepper if you wish. Then pour some oil over that. Cook in a preheated oven for about half an hour.

Satarash (*Sataraš*)

Satarash is a vegetable meal, consisting mostly of tomatoes, paprika and onions, but it is often prepared with zucchini, eggplant and carrots. Also, in some places, it is usual to add eggs and white onion. *Satarash* is a true summer meal that is a favorite throughout Bosnia and Herzegovina, Serbia and continental parts of Croatia.

Preparation Time: 30 minutes
Cooking Time: 60 minutes

Ingredients
2 tablespoons of vegetable oil
1 teaspoon of *Vegeta* or seasonal vegetables
1 teaspoon of paprika, slightly heaping
1 yellow onion, small to medium sized
1 yellow pepper
1 tomato, medium sized
1/2 cup (120 ml) of water

Preparation
Add the vegetables in this order to the cooking pan: onion, pepper and then tomato. Cut the onion into rings and then quarter the rings. It doesn't have to be chopped into small pieces, but it's totally up to you.

Heat a medium sized, non-stick skillet over medium heat until it begins to get hot. Then add the oil and let the oil sit for 30 seconds or so until it gets hot. Add the chopped-up onion and let it cook on medium heat for about 8 minutes or until it starts getting soft and translucent. While the onion is cooking, start chopping the yellow pepper into about a quarter of an inch thick strips and as long or short as you like.

Once the onion is nice and soft, add the yellow pepper. Let that cook for about 10 minutes or more, until it becomes soft. Make sure not to let the veggies burn. They should be nice and soft during the cooking process. You may need to add a little more oil if the 2 tablespoons aren't quite enough to keep everything nicely coated. Try to have enough oil in the pan to let the veggies sort of "simmer" in it. You may want to add a little water here and there, as well, to keep the sauce from getting too thick and burning onto the pan. The sauce should be thin enough to spoon onto meat and potatoes, but thick enough to keep its consistency. I usually add the water around the time the tomatoes are added.

Once the pepper starts getting soft, cut the tomato up into thick quarter inch slices. Again the size is up to you. Add to the onion and pepper mixture. Let the juices from the tomato emerge into the pan to add some more liquid. I usually lower the temperature on the stove to a nice simmering temperature at this point. You can keep the skin on the tomato and let it shrink as the tomato cooks. Once you notice that the skin starts shrinking up and almost peels away from the tomato, add the paprika, and let it cook for a few minutes to let the paprika release the flavor. Then, add *Vegeta* to taste. Add about a teaspoon, depending on how salty and flavorful you like it. Spoon over potatoes - mashed, roasted, baked, anything.

Fried Breaded Zucchini (*Pohovane tikvice*)

One of two most popular dishes with zucchini. The second version is stuffed zucchini, of course!

Preparation Time: 10 minutes
Cooking Time: 30 minutes

Ingredients
2-3 whole pieces of fresh zucchini
½ pound (230 gr) of bread crumbs
¼ pound (120 gr) of flour
2 cups (480 ml) of cooking oil
5 whole eggs
Salt according to taste
Mixed dry vegetables seasoning (optional)

Preparation
Peel 2-3 whole fresh pieces of zucchini and cut them endwise to thin slices, as many as you can get. Prepare two empty, deep soup plates and pour the bread crumbs and flour into the first plate and mix them well. Break 5 whole eggs, pour them into the second plate and whisk them well. Sprinkle each zucchini slice with salt on one side and a condiment, according to taste on the other side of the slice.

Roll each of the zucchini slice into the mixture of bread crumbs and flour, then roll it into the eggs, and roll it into the mixture of bread crumbs and flour again. This kind of treatment gives a thicker crust after the process of frying. Meanwhile, prepare a saucepan, pour in 2 cups (480 ml) of cooking oil, put it on the stove on medium, and wait for the oil to warm. Place each breaded zucchini slice into the saucepan with the hot oil. Heat the oil on medium, and when you start frying, lower the temperature down to simmer.

All sides of the zucchini slices should be fried well by turning them frequently, until they are golden brown. When the frying is complete, the fried breaded zucchini slices should be served hot, with the main meat meal (mostly with any sort of fried, breaded steaks), accompanied with French fries or mashed potatoes.

Ćevapi

The only close translation is kebab, but everyone will tell you that *ćevapi* are better. The best ones are in Bosnia and Herzegovina, and you should not miss them. However, very popular in Serbia too.

Preparation Time: 10 minutes
Cooking Time: 30 minutes

Ingredients
3 ¼ pounds (1,5 kg) of minced beef, ½ kg of minced lamb
4-5 cloves of garlic
Salt and 2 teaspoons of baking soda
Onion

Preparation
Season the meat with salt, mix it, and pour ½ cup (120 ml) of water over it with onion, which you've cooked earlier. Mix well with your hands and leave in the fridge overnight. Grind the meat in a meat grinder twice, and leave it to warm up to room temperature for a couple of hours. Then put it back in the fridge. Before you start shaping the ćevaps, mix in the baking soda. Mix well using your hands, and form into finger length sausages, about 3/4 inch (2 cm) thick. Lightly oil the grilling surface. Grill sausages until cooked through, turning as needed, about 30 minutes.

Fried Squid Rings

Preparation time: 10 minutes
Cooking time: 10 minutes

Ingredients

1 pound of frozen or fresh squid, cleaned, washed and cut to ring pieces
2 cups of cooking oil
½ pound of flour
1 tablespoon of ground red peppers
1 whole lemon, cross-cut ring slices
Salt to taste

Preparation

Pour oil into a sauce pan, turn on the stove plate to 360 F and warm up the oil. Roll the cut squid rings in the flour and red pepper powder mixture, lower the frying temperature to 300 F and fry the squid rings in the hot oil for up to 10 minutes, until they get a roasted color. Take out the roasted squid rings from the oil. Put them on previously prepared tray with paper napkins for a while to absorb some oil. Arrange fried squid rings on a serving tray with the cut lemon slices and serve them hot with french fries or a salad.

Rinflaish (*Rinflajs*)

Preparation time: 15 minutes
Cooking time: 60 minutes

Ingredients

1 pound of beef cut to medium cubes
1 ¼ pounds of whole peeled pieces of potatoes
1 ¼ cups of home cooked tomato juice
3 tablespoons of cooking oil
3 tablespoons of flour
2/3 cup of water
2 teaspoons of salt
1 teaspoon of sugar

Preparation

Wash and peel off potatoes, cut them into cubes and put them in a cooking pan. In this pan, pour enough water to cover all the potatoes and add 1 teaspoon of salt. Cook potatoes on the stove plate for about 30 minutes, until the fork goes through potatoes easily. Take the pan with the cooked potatoes from the stove plate, pour out the whole amount of water, let the potatoes cool down a bit and prepare them for serving with sauce and cooked beef.

Pour 3 tablespoons of cooking oil into a saucepan, add 3 tablespoons of flour and fry shortly, until it gets creamy. Stir constantly, preventing it from overcooking. Add tomato juice, water, 2 teaspoons of salt and sugar. Cook on a medium temperature for about 17-20 minutes, until it gets an appropriate density like any sauce. Serve hot with the cooked potatoes and cooked beef.

Roasted duck

Preparation time: 20 minutes
Cooking time: 40 minutes

Ingredients

1 whole duck, cut into pieces-parts
2-3 tablespoons of cooking oil
6-8 teaspoons of *Vegeta* or similar spice
2 ½ cups of water
Salt according to taste

Preparation

Cut one whole duck in medium parts. Take a bigger saucepan, pour in 2-3 tablespoons of cooking oil. Sprinkle salt over the duck meat according to taste, prepare and arrange the duck pieces in this saucepan. Pour in around 1 cup of water and put on a pot lid to cover the saucepan. Turn on the stove plate, put the saucepan on the plate and roast the meat on 390 F until the meat becomes soft (check it by fork tip - the fork goes through the meat easily). Add water several times during the roasting in order to prevent the roasting meat from overcooking. When the roasting is done, take the pot lid off and sprinkle 1/2 teaspoon of Vegeta over each piece of meat. Keep roasting without the pot lid for about 5 more minutes, until the meat gets reddish; then, turn each piece of meat over to the opposite side. Sprinkle a little more Vegeta over each piece of meat, wait to get reddish, and turn each piece of meat over several times. Turn off the stove plate, leave the saucepan on the hot plate for 5 minutes, turn each piece of meat over a few more times, until they all get equally reddish, and it's done.

Noodles with Ground Meat and White Sauce

Preparation time: 15 minutes
Cooking time: 60 minutes

Ingredients

1 pound of ground pork meat
1 pound of noodles
1 big onion
1 soup spoon of *Vegeta*
5-6 soup spoons of cooking oil
1 teaspoon of ground black pepper
1 teaspoon of salt
2 ½ cups of sour cream
1 egg
1 ¼ cups of classic mayonnaise
4-5 garlic cloves
8 cups of water
1 teaspoon of oregano spice
Small dose of basil

Preparation

Pour 2-3 tablespoons of cooking oil into an appropriate pan and add a bigger chopped onion, pork meat, 1 teaspoon of ground black pepper, 1 tablespoon of *Vegeta* and salt. Put the pan on the plate, turn the stove on and simmer the ground meat with its additions for about 10 minutes, with occasional stirring to prevent it from getting burnt. In the meantime, prepare noodles for cooking. Pour around 8 cups of water into another pan, add 1 soup spoon of cooking oil and cook it until it starts to boil. Pour the noodles into the boiling water and cook them for about 10 minutes, until they are done. Drain the boiled water from the pan by colander and pour the drained noodles back into the pan. Mix the braised meat with the noodles and stir it well. Put the new mixture mass into an oily (with one soup spoon of oil) refractory glass pan and add the separately prepared mixture of 1 1/14 cups of sour cream and 1 egg, stir it all well and arrange equally through the pan. Optionally, you can pour the oregano spice and basil over according to taste. Put this pan into the stove oven and bake it for about 30 minutes with the temperature of 390 F. Prepare the white sauce during the baking process. The sauce will be needed at the end, as an addition to the serving.

Pour 1 ¼ cups of sour cream, mayonnaise and 4-5 chopped garlic cloves into a glass vessel. Stir it all well and the white sauce is done. Serve with the hot baked noodles and meat, pouring over the meal on each consumer's eating plate.

Spinach Patties

Preparation time: 15 minutes
Cooking time: 25 minutes

Ingredients

1 pound of spinach
2/3 pound of potatoes
½ cup of grated hard cheese
2 cloves of garlic
½ cup of bread crumbs
1 egg
1 cup of flour
Oil for frying
Salt
Pepper

Preparation

Cook the potatoes and spinach separately in salted water. Drain, mash, stir and add the beaten egg, bread crumbs, grated cheese, mashed garlic, salt and pepper to taste. Knead the mixture to form patties. Roll them in flour and fry in hot oil until they get a rosy color.

Rice with Mushrooms

Preparation time: 10 minutes
Cooking time: 20 minutes

Ingredients

2/3 pound of mushrooms (champignons)
1 tablespoon of dried vegetable seasoning
2/3 pound of rice
1 ¼ cups of oil
2 ½ cups of sour cream
3 cups of clear soup
A pinch of oregano
Salt and pepper to taste
A bunch of parsley

Preparation

Cut mushrooms into quarters and fry them in ½ cup of oil. Add chopped parsley and dried vegetable seasoning. When mushrooms are ready, add sour cream. Heat 1 cup of oil and fry the rice, add oregano and mushrooms, stir all and pour the soup over it. Season with pepper and salt. Fry the rice over medium heat with no stirring. The rice is ready when the liquid evaporates. Serve warm.

Pork Chops with Cheese

Preparation time: 20 minutes (plus 3 hours)
Cooking time: 50 minutes

Ingredients
2 ¼ pounds of pork chops
1 pound of Trappist or any yellow cheese
3 tablespoons of mustard
4 tablespoons of béchamel sauce
2 ½ cups of sour cream
2 eggs
1 tablespoon of Parmesan cheese
Salt and pepper

Preparation
Bake chops in the oven for a short time. Chill them and remove the bones (fillets). Cut the slices almost to the end. Place the slices of meat and the slices of Trappist cheese previously smeared with mustard in an oblong baking pan. Pour the béchamel sauce up to half of the height. Leave in the refrigerator for 3 hours to become congealed. Whisk the sour cream with the eggs and pepper. Pour fillet and sprinkle parmesan cheese. Bake in pre heated oven for 45 minutes and serve warm.

Veal cooked covered with a paper sack

Preparation time: 15 minutes
Cooking time: 120 minutes

Ingredients

2 ¼ pounds of veal from shoulder
¾ pound of potatoes
2 pieces of onion
3 carrots
1 small celery root
1 parsley root
1 parsnip root water
½ cup of oil
Salt, pepper, dry basil
A laurel leaf

Preparation

Pour half of the oil in a pot and add the onion cut into slices, covering the bottom. Peel off the potato skin, cut the potatoes into fourths and place them in the pan over the onions. Cut the meat into pieces of ¾ x ¾ inch and sprinkle with salt and pepper. Place the meat pieces over the potatoes. Cut the different vegetable roots into pieces similar to the size of the meat pieces, mix them and place over the meat. Add some more dry basil, salt, pepper and a laurel leaf. Add the rest of oil and pour water, so that only the onions and potatoes are in water. Cover the pot with a wrapping paper and tie it with a piece of string. Cook at a moderate temperature until it starts to boil. Then lower the temperature to the minimum and leave it to cook for 90-100 minutes. Serve warm with milk cream.

Paprikash

Preparation time: 20 minutes
Cooking time: 60 minutes

Ingredients (5 servings)
2 ¼ pounds of raw pork ham
1 pound of potatoes
2 onions
4 tablespoons of flour
1 teaspoon of chili flakes
1 tablespoon of lard
1 tablespoon of paprika
2 carrots
Salt, pepper, parsley leaf to taste
2 tomatoes
2 eggs

Preparation
Chop onions finely and fry them in hot lard. Once onions are golden, add chopped carrots, paprika and cubed pork. Add one glass of water and simmer at medium heat for 25-30 minutes. Add water if needed. Add cubed potatoes and enough water to cover them and cook until potatoes are soft. Add tomato, seasonings and dumplings. Cook on low heat for 4-6 minutes.

Dumplings
Whisk eggs and add flour. Use a separate dish to boil about 4 ½ cups of water with a teaspoon of salt. Once the water starts boiling, use the teaspoon to form dumplings and cook them until they rise to the surface.

Lamb Roll

Preparation time: 15 minutes
Cooking time: 60 minutes

Ingredients

1/3 pound of chopped lamb meat cubes
1/3 pound of mushrooms
1 tablespoon of butter
1 chopped onion
3 tablespoons of tomatoes, chopped in cubes
1 cup of coarse grated hard cheese
1 small green pepper, chopped
10 grains of green pepper
½ cup of rose wine
1 tablespoon of parsley
1 egg yolk
1/2 package of puff pastry
Salt and pepper to taste

Preparation

Heat butter and add spices to meat and fry it. Add the finely sliced peppers, mushrooms and onions. Fry in the oil together, add the green pepper, wine and tomatoes. Continue frying and then cool it. Add cheese, parsley and piquant spices. For the roll, remove a wide strip from the thinly-made puff pastry. Put the cooled concoction on top and lay the second strip over. Attach the ends with yolk. Decorate the dough, spread with yolk and bake in a pre-heated oven for 30 minutes at 390 F degrees. Serve warm.

Roasted Trout

Preparation time: 30 minutes
Cooking time: 30 minutes

Ingredients

1 fresh trout
1 lemon
1 tablespoon of olive oil
2 cloves of garlic
Fresh parsley

Preparation

Clean trout, wash and let it drain. Chop garlic and parsley finely. There are two cloves of garlic for one trout - one for the filling and one for placing over the finished fish. Take an appropriate pan and place the parchment paper in. Brush the trout with oil on both sides and place it in the baking dish. Put the marinade of garlic, finely chopped parsley, lemon juice and olive oil on the fish. Preheat oven to 480 F and put the trout on one side for about 15 minutes, then turn and bake the other side for another 15 minutes. Pour the lemon juice, parsley and garlic.

Pork and Beef Casserole

Preparation time: 25 minutes
Cooking time: 45 minutes

Ingredients (6 servings)

2 cups of uncooked short-grain white rice
4 cups of chicken broth
1 pound of ground beef
4 pork hocks (meat removed)
1 (14.5 oz) can of drained sauerkraut
⅛ cup of olive oil
¼ cup of bacon
2 chopped onions
¼ teaspoon of salt
¼ teaspoon of pepper

Preparation

Preheat oven to 375 degrees F. Heat oil in a large skillet over medium heat and brown the onions, ground beef, bacon and pork meat from hocks. Season with salt and pepper. Stir in the rice and sauerkraut. Transfer contents to a casserole and stir in the chicken broth. Bake uncovered in a preheated oven until the rice is cooked, for around 45 minutes. Check the liquid level periodically and add water if the casserole is drying out.

Serbian Ground Beef and Vegetable Bake

Preparation time: 20 minutes
Cooking time: 70 minutes

Ingredients (4 servings)

1 pound of ground beef
1 tablespoon of olive oil
1 green bell pepper, chopped
1 chopped onion
1 shredded carrot
2 chopped celery stalks
½ tablespoon of paprika
½ teaspoon of salt
¾ teaspoon of black pepper
¼ teaspoon of crushed red pepper
1 pinch of ground cinnamon
1 pinch of ground cloves
¼ cup of water
1/8 cup of red wine
1 cube of beef bouillon
2 tablespoons of half-and-half
2 peeled and sliced potatoes

Preparation

Preheat the oven to 400 F. Lightly grease a casserole dish. Cook the beef in a skillet over medium heat, until evenly brown and then remove from the skillet. Reserve the juices and set them aside. Mix in the olive oil and sauté the green pepper, carrot, onion and celery until tender. Return the beef to the skillet and season with salt, black and red pepper, paprika, cinnamon and cloves. Stir in the water and red wine until heated through. Dissolve the beef bouillon cube into the mixture. Remove the skillet from heat and mix in the half-and-half. Layer the bottom of the prepared casserole dish with enough potato slices to cover. Place the beef and the vegetable mixture over the potatoes and top with the remaining potatoes. Cook covered for 45 minutes in the preheated oven, or until the potatoes are tender.

Traditional Serbian Burger (*Pljeskavica*)

Preparation time: 15 minutes
Cooking time: 20 minutes

Ingredients (4 servings)
1 pound of ground beef
1 pound of ground pork
½ teaspoon of black pepper
½ cup of sparkling water
1 teaspoon of sweet paprika
2 tablespoons of olive oil
2 teaspoons of salt
2 medium onions, finely chopped
Ajvar (see the recipe for homemade ajvar in this cookbook)
Vegetable oil
4 pita breads
Onions and pickles to taste

Preparation
In a bowl, mix ground pork and beef, sweet paprika, black pepper, salt and sparkling water with hands. Brush olive oil on the surface of the meat mixture. Cover with a plastic wrap and refrigerate for at least a 150 minutes. Add the onions to the meat mixture and mix well. Divide into 4 balls and use your hands to pound it to a thin patty. The size should be about 7 inches in diameter for each *pljeskavica*. Grill or fry your patties for about 3-4 minutes per side or more, if desired. Take pita pockets and assemble your burgers by spreading *ajvar* and *kajmak* and adding onions and pickles.

Turkey with Rice

Preparation time: 20 minutes
Cooking time: 40 minutes

Ingredients (4 servings)

1 pound of turkey breast fillet
2 red bell peppers
2 onions
2 garlic cloves
2 tablespoons of canola oil
Salt and pepper
1 teaspoon of sweet paprika
1 teaspoon of paprika
7 ounces of long-grain rice
2 tablespoons of tomato paste
1 ¼ pints of poultry broth
14 oz of canned whole tomatoes, peeled

Preparation

Rinse the turkey breast fillet, pat dry and cut into 3/4 inch cubes. Cut bell peppers into quarters, remove the seeds, rinse and dice. Peel the onions and garlic and chop finely. Heat the oil in a heavy pot and brown the meat over high heat. Season with salt and pepper, while adding the onions, garlic and bell peppers to the pot. Cook for 1 more minute and sprinkle with paprika. Add rice and stir in the tomato paste. Add broth and diced tomatoes and bring to a boil. Cover and cook over medium heat, stirring frequently for 20 minutes. Season meat with salt and pepper and serve immediately.

Spiced Pork and Potatoes with Rice

Preparation time: 20 minutes
Cooking time: 40 minutes

Ingredients (4 servings)

1 ¾ pounds of pork shoulder

2 onions

2 garlic cloves

½ pound of waxy potatoes

2 tomatoes

2 tablespoons of clarified butter

2 tablespoons of ground paprika (sweet)

1 teaspoon of ground paprika (hot)

5 cups of beef broth

Salt

Freshly ground pepper

1 shallot

1 teaspoon of butter

1/2 pound of long-grain rice

1/3 cup of grated cheese (such as Gouda)

2 tablespoons of freshly chopped parsley

Preparation

Rinse pork, pat dry and cut into small cubes. Peel and finely chop the garlic and onions. Peel and dice the potatoes. Blanch tomatoes in boiling water and rinse with cold water, then peel, core, quarter and dice. Fry the onions and garlic in a pan in melted butter until translucent. Add the pork and fry until golden-brown. Add tomatoes, potatoes, and paprika. Deglaze with about approximately 2 cups of broth. Cover and simmer for about 30 minutes over medium heat. Season with salt and pepper. Finely chop the shallot. In a pan, sauté shallot in butter. Add the rice and the remaining broth. Cover and simmer for 20 minutes over low heat. Mix the rice with meat and season to taste. Serve sprinkled with cheese and parsley.

Raznjici

Preparation time: 15 minutes
Cooking time: 20 minutes

Ingredients (4 servings)

2/3 pound of pork meat

½ red pepper (small)

½ green pepper (small)

½ onion (small)

3 ½ ounces of bacon (cured)

2 pinches of ground black pepper

3 pinches of salt

2 tablespoons of oil (olive or plain salad oil)

Preparation

Cut the meat, peppers, onions and bacon into bite size squares. Arrange cut ingredients on wooden sticks. Pour oil in a grill pan and pan roast for about 11-16 minutes until golden brown. In the process of roasting, add salt and pepper.

Vegetarian Pilaf

Preparation time: 10 minutes
Cooking time: 20 minutes

Ingredients

1 cup of rice
1 medium carrot, grated
1 big red bell pepper, diced
1 teaspoon of sweet paprika
1 big onion, diced
¼ teaspoon of ground pepper
2 tablespoons of oil
3 cups of water
Sea salt to taste

Preparation

Heat the oil in a large pan. Add the chopped onion and sauté for 3 minutes. Add the diced pepper and grated carrot, as well as rice, along with 3 cups of water. Stir until all ingredients are evenly spread. Add salt, pepper and paprika and let it boil for 5 minutes over medium heat. Remove from the heat and cover with a lid. Let it rest for up to 15 minutes, until all water is absorbed by the rice. Garnish and serve.

Fish Skewers with Relish

Preparation time: 10 minutes
Cooking time: 25 minutes

Ingredients (6 servings)
2 pounds of fish steaks or 2 pounds of fillets, skinned and boned
1 tablespoon of olive oil
2 garlic cloves, minced
1/4 teaspoon of pepper
Vegetable oil cooking spray
2 large tomatoes
1 medium onion, finely chopped
1 small red hot chili pepper, seeded and finely chopped
1 small green hot chili pepper, seeded and finely chopped
1 small yellow hot chili pepper, seeded and finely chopped
1 teaspoon of sugar
1 tablespoon of red wine vinegar

Preparation
Core, peel and dice the tomatoes, combine with onion, sugar, red, yellow and green hot chili peppers and wine vinegar. Stir until well combined. Cover and refrigerate for at least 30 minutes.

Cut fish into 1 1/2-inch chunks. Mix pepper, oil and garlic. Add fish pieces, turning lightly to coat on all sides. Thread onto 6 skewers. Spray the broiler rack with the cooking spray. Place the skewers on the rack about 5 inches from heat. Broil, turning carefully to cook on all sides. Cook and turn until lightly browned, for up to 12 minutes. Serve with tomato relish.

Chicken Burger (Pileća Pljeskavica)

Preparation time: 15 minutes
Cooking time: 20 minutes

Ingredients

1 chicken leg
1 cucumber
1 carrot
1 bun
1 pavlaka or a similar product
1 paprika
Kajmak (see the separate recipe in this cookbook)
Soft cheese
Forest spring onions
Salt and pepper

Preparation

Remove the bones from the chicken leg and sprinkle with salt and pepper. Slice the cucumber and grate the carrot. Marble together *kajmak* and the soft cheese along with the paprika. Preheat the pan, oil it up.

Cook the chicken legs until golden brown. Cut the bun in half, warm it on coals, and then cover with *pavlaka*. Chop a handful of forest spring onions, place them on *pavlaka* and add some carrot strips. Pour it with sauce left in the pan.

Vege Sarma (*Posna Sarma*)

Preparation time: 15 minutes
Cooking time: 80 minutes

Ingredients (4 servings)

1 cabbage or sweet cabbage
1 green pepper, diced
1 1/5 cups of cooked rice
5 diced onions
1 1/5 cups of ground walnuts
2 stalks of celery
Olive oil
1 can of whole tomatoes
Salt

Preparation

Cut out the hard core of the cabbage and boil it, then separate each leaf. Heat oil in a skillet and add the celery, onions, and green pepper. Fry until soft, add the cooked rice and stir fry the mixture for 2-3 minutes. Remove the mixture from heat and add walnuts and salt. Mix well.

Take a cabbage leaf and scoop a tablespoon of the mixture on it. Roll up the leaf, the sides should be folded inside to prevent the mixture from falling out. Place the rolls in a large pan, add the tomatoes and enough water to cover them. Cook over a medium heat for 55-70 minutes. Keep the pan covered during the cooking process, until serving.

Salads

Serbian Salad

Difference between *Srpska* and *Shopska*? Shopska is with and Serbian is without cheese.

Preparation time: 15 minutes

Ingredients (4 servings)
Salad
3 vine-ripened tomatoes
1 cucumber
1 green bell pepper
Red onions, to taste

Dressing
Red wine vinegar
Olive oil
¼ teaspoon of dried oregano
Salt
Pepper

Preparation
Toss all salad ingredients together. Drizzle with vinegar, oil and seasonings.

Salad with red beet and carrot

Preparation time: 15 minutes

Ingredients

2/3 pound of carrot

2/3 pound of beet

2 cloves of garlic

Several leaves of fresh mint

Vinegar made of plums

Oil

Salt

Pepper

Preparation

Grate the raw carrots and beets. Add finely chopped garlic and several leaves of fresh mint. Stir well and add oil, plum vinegar, salt and pepper. Serve decorated with fresh mint.

The Potato Salad (*Krompir salata*)

Preparation time: 20 minutes
Cooking time: 30 minutes

Ingredients (4 servings)
2 average pieces of onion
1 tablespoon of oil
2 teaspoons of vinegar
½ teaspoon of pepper
1 teaspoon of salt

Preparation
Wash and cook the whole unpeeled potatoes in hot boiling water for about 25-30 minutes. Clean the onions and cut them into small thin slices. Put the onion slices into a deeper and wider dish, add some salt according to taste and leave it for some time (about 60 minutes). Pour the vinegar, oil and pepper into the separate dish and whisk well.

When the potatoes are cooked, peel them and cut them into ring slices, about 1/5 inch thick. Put the potato ring slices into the dish with onions, cover it with vinegar, oil and pepper from the separate dish. Whisk it all well carefully not to break the potato ring slices and so that they keep their shape intact as much as possible.

Rice and Vegetable Salad

Preparation time: 10 minutes
Cooking time: 15 minutes

Ingredients

1/2 pound of rice
2 red bell peppers
2/3 cup of black olives
2 tablespoons of capers
3 pickled cucumbers
2 yellow bell peppers
2 green bell peppers
3 carrots
2 tomatoes
4 tablespoons of oil
Juice of 2 lemons
Salt and paper to taste

Preparation

Cook the rice in salted water, drain and wash with cold water. Cook the carrots until soft. Chop the bell peppers, pickled cucumbers, carrots, olives and tomatoes without seeds into cubes. Add the capers, lemon juice, oil, salt and pepper. Slowly stir the rice with everything and serve cold.

Homemade Salad

Preparation time: 10 minutes

Ingredients
2 ¼ pounds of cheese
½ pound of chopped deli meat
5 pickled gherkins, finely grated
3 onions, finely grated
5 boiled eggs, coarse grated
1 tablespoon of mayonnaise
3-4 tablespoons of *ajvar* (please see the separate recipe in this cookbook)
Salt and pepper to taste

Preparation
Mix all the ingredients together. Leave in the fridge for a little while and then enjoy the salad.

Lettuce with sour milk

Preparation time: 15 minutes

Ingredients

1 piece of lettuce

2/3 cup of walnuts

1 cup of sour milk

Several cloves of garlic

1 tea spoonful of fennel

1 bundle of green (spring) onions

Salt, vinegar, oil

Preparation

Wash the lettuce, let it dry a bit and tear into pieces, mix it with the chopped garlic, green onions and coarsely ground walnuts. Add salt, oil, vinegar and mix well. Pour the sour milk over it before serving.

Shopska salad

Preparation time: 10 minutes

Ingredients
¼ pound of hard cheese (feta is fine too, but then you have Greek salad)

2 tomatoes

1 medium cucumber

2 fresh peppers

1 teaspoon of olive oil

Salt

Preparation
Wash peppers, tomatoes and cucumbers. Peel the cucumbers, cut them lengthwise into quarters and horizontally thin. Cut the peppers to thin circles and tomatoes into smaller pieces. Season to taste. Add a teaspoon of olive oil and stir everything well. Mash the cheese with a fork and sprinkle it on top of the salad.

Cucumber Salad

Preparation time: 15 minutes

Ingredients

3 fresh cucumbers
1 teaspoon of vinegar
3 tablespoons of sour cream
1 teaspoon of salt
2/3 teaspoon of sugar
3 average cloves of garlic

Preparation

Peel the cucumbers and cut them into thin round slices with a slicer. Squeeze water out of them by hand and pour the squeezed water out. Add salt, sugar and garlic. Add a teaspoon of vinegar and stir it well. Add the sour cream, stir it all well once more, distribute the finished salad into several dishes, arrange and decorate.

Minted Romaine Salad

Preparation time: 15 minutes

Ingredients

1 medium-sized piece of romaine

¼ cup of sliced scallions, with some tops

2 hard-boiled eggs, shelled and sliced

½ cup of walnuts, chopped

2 tablespoons of fresh mint, chopped

¼ cup of olive oil

2 tablespoons of fresh lemon juice

Salt and pepper to taste

Preparation

Wash the romaine and separate the leaves. Break them into bite-size pieces, dry thoroughly and refrigerate. When ready to serve, put the romaine pieces in a salad bowl. Add the eggs, scallions, walnuts, and mint and toss lightly. Combine the remaining ingredients and pour over the salad. Toss again and serve at once.

Pepper mashing salad

Preparation time: 35 minutes
Baking time: 20 minutes

Ingredients (5 servings)
4 large red peppers
3 tomatoes
1 clove of garlic
Salt, oil and parsley leaf

Preparation
Bake the peppers, drain, peel and chop finely. Also finely chop the garlic and tomatoes. Place all the ingredients in an appropriate dish and ground them with a wooden pestle. Season with salt and pepper. Serve cool, after decorating with parsley leaf.

Desserts

Vanilice

These desserts are small and not very fancy. No one knows why they are so popular. *Vanilice* are definitely one of the simplest and most popular cookies in Serbia and the Balkans.

Preparation Time: 20 minutes
Cooking Time: 50 minutes

Ingredients

2 1/3 pounds (1 kg) of flour
1 pound (450 gr) of lard
1 cup (240 ml) of yogurt
1 cup (230 gr) of sugar
3 packages of vanilla sugar
Confectioners' sugar
Plum or apricot jam

Preparation

Use a mixer to mix the lard with the sugar in a bowl, then add the yogurt. Gradually add the flour and make a smooth dough. Dust the workspace with some flour and then spread the dough until it is 0,2 inch (5 mm) thick. Using a small glass, stamp out the cookies (round shape), and place them in a tray covered with baking sheets. Preheat the oven to 300°F (150°C) and bake the vanilice for about 15 minutes. Make sure they don't turn too golden. After they cool, take one cookie at a time, spread it with jam and top it with another cookie. Finally, roll each cookie in the vanilla sugar generously.

Baklava

Baklava is flaky, crisp and tender. You will love the hint of mellow lemon flavor, which offsets the sweetness and compliments the cinnamon. It's truly delicious. This baklava recipe is well loved wherever it goes, it is definitely a favorite.

Preparation Time: 60 minutes
Cooking Time: 75 minutes

Ingredients

1 pound (450 gr) of package phyllo (filo) dough, thawed according to the package instructions2 1/2 sticks (1/4 cup or 290 gr) of melted unsalted butter
1 pound (450 gr) of walnuts, finely chopped
1 tablespoon of ground cinnamon
1 cup (230 gr) of granulated sugar
2 tablespoons of lemon juice (juice of 1/2 lemon)
3/4 cup (180 ml) of water
1/2 cup (120 ml) of honey
Melted chocolate chips and chopped walnuts for garnish (optional)

Preparation

Thaw the phyllo dough according to the package instructions (it is best to do this overnight and leave it in the fridge. Place it on the counter for 1 hour, before starting the cooking process to bring it to room temperature). Trim the phyllo dough to fit your baking sheet. The best phyllo dough package contains 2 rolls, with a total of 40 sheets that measure 9×14, so you have to trim them slightly. You can trim one stack at a time, then cover with a damp towel to keep the dough from drying out.

Butter the bottom and the sides of a 13×9 non-stick baking pan. In a medium saucepan, combine 1 cup (230 gr) of sugar, 1/2 cup (120 ml) of honey, 2 tablespoons of lemon juice, and 3/4 cup (180ml) of water. Bring to a boil over medium high heat, stirring until the sugar dissolves, then reduce the heat to medium low and boil for an additional 4 minutes without stirring. Remove from heat, and let the syrup cool while preparing the filling.

Preheat the oven to 325°F (160°C). Pulse the walnuts for about 10 times in a food processor until coarsely ground/finely chopped. In a medium bowl, stir together: 1 pound (450 gr) of finely chopped walnuts and 1 tablespoon of cinnamon. Place 10 phyllo sheets in the baking pan one at a time, brushing each sheet with butter once it's in the pan, before adding the next one (i.e. place a phyllo sheet in the pan, brush the top with butter, place the next phyllo sheet in the pan, butter the top etc.)

Keep the remaining phyllo covered with a damp towel at all times. Spread about 1/5 of the nut mixture (about 3/4 cup) over the phyllo dough. Add 5 buttered sheets of phyllo, then another layer of nuts. Repeat 4 times.Finish off with 10 layers of buttered phyllo sheets. Brush the top with butter. Here's the order:

10 buttered phyllo sheets, 3/4 cup (180 gr) of nut mixture,
5 buttered phyllo sheets, 3/4 cup (180 gr) of nut mixture,
5 buttered phyllo sheets, 3/4 cup (180 gr) of nut mixture,
5 buttered phyllo sheets, 3/4 cup (180 gr) of nut mixture,
5 buttered phyllo sheets, 3/4 cup (180 gr) of nut mixture
10 buttered phyllo sheets and butter on top

Cut pastry into 1 1/2" wide strips, then cut diagonally to form diamond shapes. Bake at 325°F (160°C) for 1 hour and 15 min or until the top is golden brown. Remove from the oven and immediately spoon the chilled syrup evenly over the hot baklava (you'll hear it sizzle). This will ensure that it stays crisp rather than soggy. Let the baklava cool completely, uncovered and at a room temperature. For the best results, let baklava sit for 4-6 hours or overnight at a room temperature for the syrup to penetrate and soften the layers. Garnish baklava with finely chopped nuts or drizzle with melted chocolate. Store at a room temp, covered with a tea towel for up to 2 weeks.

Balkan Doughnuts (*Krofne*)

Some doughnuts recipes call for unseasoned mashed potatoes in the dough, but not this one. Compare this recipe with other doughnuts around the globe.

Preparation Time: 60 minutes
Cooking Time: 30 minutes

Ingredients

1 cup (240 ml) of scalded milk
4 ounces/1 stick of butter
1/4 cup (50gr) of sugar
2 teaspoons of salt
1 package of yeast (active dry)
1 cup (240ml) of water
3 large eggs (room-temperature, slightly beaten)
6 cups (1,3 kg) of flour (all-purpose)
4 cups (960 ml) of cooking oil (for frying)
Granulated or confectioners' sugar

Preparation

Scald 1 cup (240 ml) of milk and add 4 ounces of butter, 1/4 cup (50 gr) of sugar and 2 teaspoons of salt, stirring to melt the butter. Cool to 110°F (42°C). Meanwhile, dissolve 1 package (2 1/4 teaspoons) of active dry yeast in 1 cup of 110°F (42°C) water.

Place the milk mixture, yeast mixture and 3 large, slightly beaten room-temperature eggs in a large bowl or a stand mixer fitted with the dough hook, mixing until smooth. Add 6 cups of all-purpose flour gradually, mixing until smooth. The dough might be sticky. If so, use slightly dampened hands to transfer it to a greased bowl (don't add more flour). Cover and let rise until doubled. For extra-light *krofne*, some cooks punch down the dough and let it rise a second time until doubled.

Punch down the dough and roll it on a lightly floured work surface to a ½ inch (1,2 cm) thickness. Cut with a 3-inch round cutter or glass and let rise, covered, for about half an hour. Heat oil to 375°F (190°C) in a heavy-bottomed pot or a Dutch oven. Use a deep-frying thermometer to make sure the temperature is accurate. Fry *krofne* in hot oil until lightly brown on both sides, turning only once. Place on an absorbent paper. While still hot, roll in granulated sugar or dust with confectioners' sugar.

Tulumbe

This very popular dessert exists everywhere in the Balkans, but the most popular versions are definitely in Albania, Kosovo, Turkey and Bosnia and Herzegovina.

Preparation Time: 15 minutes
Cooking Time: 30 minutes

Ingredients
Pastry
2 tablespoons of butter or 2 tablespoons of margarine, melted
1 cup (230 gr) of flour
3 tablespoons of water
4 eggs
1/2 teaspoon of salt
1 1/4 cups (300 ml) of olive oil, for frying

Syrup
2 cups (460 gr) of sugar
1 3/4 cups (420 ml) of water
1 teaspoon of lemon juice

Preparation
Syrup
Put the sugar, water and lemon juice into a saucepan and after the sugar is melted by stirring, allow the syrup to boil until moderately thick. Set aside to cool.

Pastry

Heat the margarine in a saucepan, add the water and salt and bring to a boil. Reduce the heat and add the flour at once. Stir the mixture constantly with a wooden spoon and continue until the mixture pulls away from the sides of the pan and forms a ball. This should take 6 minutes. Then remove the pan from the heat and set aside to cool. When cool, add the eggs and knead for approximately 10 minutes. Using a pastry bag with a large nozzle or a serrated spoon, put 7-8 pastries in a pan containing the heated olive oil. Start frying the pastry over low heat, increase the heat when the pastry puffs up a bit, and fry until golden. Remove the fried pastry with a slotted spoon, draining away the oil, and then put into the syrup. Strain off the syrup, place the tulumba on a serving plate and serve when cool.

Koh

I have never met any kid in the Serbia that dislikes *koh*. It is nice, delicious, and always reminds us of our childhood.

Preparation Time: 15 minutes
Cooking Time: 30 minutes

Ingredients
6 eggs
4 cups (960 ml) of milk
12 tablespoons of sugar
12 tablespoons of semolina
2 packages of vanilla sugar

Preparation
Whisk the egg whites until they form a soft peak. Add 6 tablespoons of sugar, egg yolks, semolina and 1 package of vanilla sugar. Pour the batter into a greased and floured baking dish. Bake at 400°F (200°C) until golden on top. Boil milk with 6 tablespoons of sugar and vanilla sugar. While the cake is still hot, pour the milk over it. Cool it and serve.

Ice Cubes

Preparation time: 15 minutes
Cooking time: 45 minutes

Ingredients

Custard topping

3 cups of milk

2/3 cup of sugar

1 tablespoon of vanilla extract

2/3 cup of all-purpose flour

16 tablespoons of softened unsalted butter (2 sticks)

Cake

1/3 cup of unsweetened cocoa powder

1/3 cup of all-purpose flour

½ teaspoon of baking powder

6 separated eggs

1/3 cup of sugar

Butter for greasing

Syrup

1 cup of sugar

1 cup of water

½ teaspoon of rose water

Chocolate topping

8 oz of semi-sweet chocolate

1/3 cup of vegetable oil

Preparation

Custard topping

Heat up the milk, sugar and vanilla extract until steaming. Meanwhile, ladle enough milk into the flour to create a thick slurry. Pour it back into the milk mixture and heat until it resembles a thick vanilla pudding. Be sure to whisk well, not to form lumps. Let it cool completely, then whisk in the butter.

Cake

Preheat the oven to 350 F. Grease a 13×9 cake pan generously with butter. In a large bowl, whisk together the baking powder, cocoa and flour. Beat the egg whites until foamy, then gradually add the sugar until glossy, stiff peaks form. Fold in the egg yolks. Fold the cocoa mixture into the egg white mixture. Spread the thick, fluffy brown cocoa batter into the cake pan. Bake for about 25 minutes.

Syrup

Simmer the sugar, water and orange blossom water until the sugar dissolves, about 5 minutes. Then, use a fork to poke a few holes on the cake. Pour the syrup over the hot cake. Let it sit until completely absorbed.

Chocolate topping

Melt the chocolate over a double boiler and stir in the oil. Set aside to cool until lukewarm.

Assemble

Top the cake with the chilled custard cream, spreading it out evenly with a spatula. Pour on the chocolate topping and smooth it out. Dust on some cocoa powder if you don't want to mess with the chocolate. Refrigerate the cake overnight to set the chocolate, then slice it into neat squares.

Gurabije

Preparation time: 20 minutes
Cooking time: 30 minutes

Ingredients

6 cups of flour

2 eggs

1 pack of baking powder

½ cup of oil

A pinch of soda

2 1/2 cups of sugar

2/3 cup of yogurt or sour milk

1 cup of apple syrup

Preparation

Make the dough out of all the ingredients. It should be elastic and not sticky to hands. Add some more flour if needed. Make about 50 balls from the dough. Flatten each ball to be ½ inch thick. Dent a lump of sugar into each. Put them in a baking mould and pour the apple syrup over them. Bake them at 360 F until they become yellow brownish. Leave them to cool and pour some more apple syrup on the biscuits before serving.

Urmashice

Preparation time: 15 minutes
Cooking time: 25 minutes

Ingredients
Dough
1/3 pound of sugar
1 cup of oil
1 pound of flour
1 pack of baking powder
1/3 cup of walnuts

Syrup
1 ½ pounds of sugar
2 cups of water

Preparation
Combine all the dough ingredients to form soft and not sticky dough. If needed, add some more flour. Make walnut size balls from the dough. Insert a half of a walnut into each ball and make a proper shape with hands. Optionally, you can make a pattern with a fork on the surface. Place them on a baking tray and bake at 390 F till they get a golden yellow color. While the cookies are baked, make a syrup from the sugar and water in a pan. Optionally you can add several drops of lemon juice. While the cookies are warm, pour the syrup over them and leave them to cool.

Serbian Crepes

Preparation time: 10 minutes
Cooking time: 15 minutes

Ingredients (2 servings)

1 cup all-purpose flour
2 large eggs
1 egg yolk
¾ cup of whole milk
1 teaspoon of vanilla
2 tablespoons of chilled melted butter
2 tablespoons of sugar or less
A pinch of salt
¾ cup of water
1 teaspoon of oil to brush the pan
Whipped cream, Nutella, jam to taste

Preparation

In a medium mixing bowl whisk together the milk, vanilla, flour, eggs and an additional yolk, butter, sugar and salt, forming a thick, smooth batter. Add water and refrigerate for 1 hour if possible. Heat a 9-inch crepe pan (ceramic recommended) on medium heat. When hot, brush the pan with oil for the first crepe (optional). Pour 3 to 4 ounces of the batter into the center of the pan with a ladle, quickly rotating the pan to cover its surface. Add more batter to fill any holes. Cook until the edges are firm, the batter slightly bubbled and opaque, and the bottom is lightly browned. Flip the crepe and cook the other side, adjusting the heat as needed. Transfer to a warmed plate and cook the remaining crepes. Place a tablespoon of filling in each crepe and roll or fold in quarters. Serve warm, drizzled with Nutella, jam or whipped cream as desired.

Serbian Apple Pita (*Pita sa Jabukama*)

Preparation time: 15 minutes
Cooking time: 45 minutes

Ingredients

¾ cup of sugar
4 pounds of peeled and chopped Granny Smith apples
Juice of 1 lemon
2 1-pound packages of phyllo dough
½ pound (2 sticks) of unsalted melted butter
¾ cup of uncooked farina (i.e. Cream of Wheat)
1 teaspoon of cinnamon
¾ cup of chopped walnuts
Powdered sugar for sprinkling on top

Preparation

Preheat the oven to 375 degrees. Prepare the filling by mixing the sugar, farina, cinnamon and walnuts, if using. Add the apples and the lemon juice, tossing lightly to coat the apples. Place 1 sheet of phyllo dough on the cutting board, portrait-style. Using a pastry brush, brush with melted butter. Place 1 large serving spoon of the mixture (about 3 ounces) in the middle of the phyllo dough and fold the sides for about 3 inches, so that they touch in the middle. Roll up like a burrito. Repeat this process with each phyllo sheet. Brush each roll with butter and place on the baking sheet. Bake for about 35-40 minutes or until golden brown. Sprinkle with powdered sugar before serving.

Orehnjacha

Preparation time: 30 minutes

Cooking time: 45 minutes

Ingredients (40 servings)

Dough

2 tablespoons of active dry yeast

1 tablespoon of sugar (white)

1/2 cup of water (110 F)

1 (12-ounce) can of evaporated milk

4 large beaten eggs

7 1/2 cups of all-purpose flour

4 tablespoons of white sugar

1 teaspoon of salt

8 ounces of cold butter

Filling

2 1/2 pounds of ground, not chopped walnuts

2 cups of white sugar

1 to 2 cups of scalded milk

Egg Wash

1 to 2 large eggs (beaten with 1 teaspoon of water per egg used)

Preparation

Dough

In a medium bowl, dissolve the yeast and 1 tablespoon of sugar in warm water. Add the evaporated milk and 4 beaten eggs, mix well. Set aside. In a large bowl, mix together the flour, 4 tablespoons of sugar, and salt. Cut in the butter with fingers until crumbly. Add the liquid ingredients and continue mixing by hand until a smooth dough forms. Shape the dough into a ball, cover with the mixing bowl, and let rise until doubled. Divide the dough into 5 balls, cover and let it rise again until doubled.

Filling

Mix together the ground walnuts (they should look like sawdust), sugar and the scalded milk.

Let cool to room temperature, stirring occasionally.

Assembling

Working with one ball of the dough at a time, roll them out to 1/8-inch thickness. You shouldn't need additional flour for rolling. Spread with 1/5 of the walnut filling. Roll from the bottom up (or top down, if you prefer) and tuck in the ends. Place them seam-side down on a parchment-lined sheet pan. Cover with a greased plastic wrap and let rise until almost doubled.

Heat the oven to 325 F. Pierce the nut roll several times with a fork down its length and then brush with egg wash. Bake the rolls for about 30 to 40 minutes or until golden on top and bottom. Cool completely on a wire rack. Nut rolls can be served as is or dusted with confectioners' sugar.

Serbian Multi-Layered Chocolate Cream Cake (Reforma torta)

Preparation time: 30 minutes

Cooking time: 60 minutes

Ingredients (10 servings)

Walnut Sponge Cake

10 large egg whites

2 1/2 cups of sugar

10.5 ounces of ground, not chopped walnuts

2 tablespoons of dry bread crumbs (or dry cake crumbs)

Chocolate Cream Filling

8 ounces of chopped chocolate

2 ounces of unsweetened chocolate, chopped

1 pound/4 sticks of unsalted butter, softened

5 large egg whites

1 cup of granulated sugar

Preparation

Walnut Sponge

Place a rack in the middle of the oven and heat it to 350 F. Lightly butter four 9x3-inch loaf pans and line the bottoms with parchment paper. Whip the egg whites until stiff. Slowly add the sugar and whip again to stiff peaks. Mix the breadcrumbs with walnuts and gently fold into the egg whites until well incorporated. Divide the batter evenly among prepared loaf pans and bake for about 8 to 13 minutes, or until the center springs back when lightly pressed and the edges are just beginning to color. Remove from the oven and cool in pan for 3-4 minutes. Run a knife around the edge of the sponge cake to loosen it. Carefully invert onto a cooling rack and peel off the parchment paper. Let it cool completely and then split each sponge cake in half horizontally, so that you have 8 layers.

Filling

Melt the chocolate in a microwave and set aside to cool to room temperature. In a large bowl, beat the butter on low for 2 minutes, then on medium for 3 minutes and finally on high for 5 minutes. Place the egg whites and sugar in a double boiler over medium heat. Transfer to a mixing bowl and whip on high until stiff peaks form. Fold the melted chocolate into the whipped butter, then gently fold in the egg whites until all traces of white are gone. Refrigerate until ready to use.

Assemble

Place one layer of walnut sponge on a serving tray and spread a layer of chocolate filling on it. Repeat the process until all eight layers are stacked on top of each other. Frost the top and the sides of the cake with the remaining chocolate filling. If desired, garnish with a sprinkle of chopped walnuts, but this is not necessary.

Vasa's cake (*Vasina torta*)

Preparation time: 30 minutes
Cooking time: 100 minutes

Ingredients

Biscuit
5 egg whites
1 tablespoon of soft flour
½ cup of ground almonds
½ cup of rind chocolate for cooking
5 tablespoons of crystal sugar
5 yolks

White cream
4 egg whites
½ pound of sugar
2/3 cup of water

Filling
4 egg yolks
10 tablespoons of orange juice
1 orange, finely rind peel
1/3 pound of butter, softened at room temperature
4 tablespoons of crystal sugar
½ cup of milk
1 ½ cups of crystal sugar
2 ½ cups of ground walnuts
½ cup of melted chocolate for cooking

Preparation

Biscuit

Whisk the egg whites with a mixer; gradually add the sugar spoon by spoon, whisking until a creamy and light structure is obtained. Whisk the egg yolks separately and add them into the egg whites mixture slowly and mix with a wooden spoon. Mix in the nuts, flour and grated chocolate and gently mix with a wooden spoon. We need to maintain the light structure as much as possible. Cover the bottom of a cake mold (with a diameter of 10 inch) with baking paper and coat the edges of the mold with butter. Pour in the mixture, flatten it slightly and bake at 390 F for about 20-30 minutes. Allow the crust to cool in the pan. Separate the edges of the baking tray with a knife and remove the biscuit from the mold. Remove the paper and put the biscuit on a serving plate.

Filling

Whisk the egg yolks with 4 tablespoons of sugar for a little while, then let them simmer for about 5 minutes. Leave them to cool. The yolks will cook briefly because of the heat treatment only, so they do not need to be cooked for more than 10 minutes, unlike for other cakes. Heat the milk with 1 cup of sugar and pour it over the nuts. The amount of milk depends on the dryness of the nuts. Add the melted chocolate, orange peel and the orange juice to the lukewarm mixture. Allow the chocolate filling to cool. Whisk the butter with the mixer and combine with the cooked cooled egg yolks and chocolate filling, whisking with the mixer for about 1 minute to make the filling airy and light. Apply the filling evenly only on the top of the biscuit, not on the sides, and put it in the fridge to cool well.

The cream

Boil the sugar with water for about 20 minutes, or until it thickens and begins to have a consistency of honey. Whisk the egg whites with a mixer, then gradually add the boiled water and sugar to the egg whites and continue to mix for about 5 minutes. Apply the white cream over the cake and put in the fridge again for several hours.

Floating island (*Shnenokle*)

Preparation time: 15 minutes
Cooking time: 15 minutes

Ingredients (5 servings)
5 eggs
4 1/3 cups of milk
6 tablespoons of sugar
2 tablespoons of vanilla sugar
2 tablespoons of flour

Preparation
Add one tablespoon of vanilla sugar into milk and let it simmer at low heat. At the same time whisk the egg whites into thick foam, add 2 tablespoons of sugar and whisk until the sugar has melted. Dip a spoon in the milk and then make egg-white dumplings. Cook them for a short time at low heat and transfer them to a bowl or separate small bowls with a slotted spoon. As they are cooking, baste them with surrounding milk so they are evenly done. Whisk the egg yolks and the remaining sugar in a bowl, add hot milk used to cook the dumplings, return this mixture into the dish and cook a custard cream. Pour the custard over the dumplings.

Dobosh cake

Preparation time: 30 minutes
Cooking time: 25 minutes

Ingredients (5 servings)

Crust sheets
8 eggs
8 tablespoons of flour
6 tablespoons of sugar
grated lemon zest

Glaze
1 cup of sugar
1 tablespoon of water

Filling
2 cups of butter
2 egg yolks
2 cups of sugar
1 cup of chocolate
1 teaspoon of vanilla sugar
5 tablespoons of water

Preparation

Crust Sheets
First whisk the egg whites to foam. Separately whisk the egg yolks with sugar until they change color to a whiter shade. Add some grated lemon zest. Combine the egg yolks and whites and gradually add flour. The crusts should be baked briefly, for about 5 minutes, at 360 F. Baking trays should be well-greased and dusted with flour or lined with baking paper.

Filling

Simmer water, sugar, chocolate and vanilla sugar on low heat with constant mixing until the liquid boils. Remove from heat and mix until the filling cools. Add butter and 2 whisked egg yolks and mix well. All crusts, except one, should be coated with the filling, while some filling should be left for coating the sides and for decoration.

Glaze

Mix sugar with a little water, until the sugar is just moist. Cook until the sugar melts completely and then caramelizes (light golden). Pour the hot sugar mixture over the last crust and cut the cake with hot knife.

Lazy pie (Lenja pita)

Preparation time: 20 minutes
Cooking time: 45 minutes

Ingredients (5 servings)
Dough
2 cups of flour
1 teaspoon of baking powder
1 cup of sugar
1 cup of milk
1/2 cup of oil
1 egg

Filling
3 1/3 pounds of apples
1 tablespoon of cinnamon
1 teaspoon of vanilla sugar
1 cup of sugar

Preparation
Peel and grate the apples. Add sugar, vanilla sugar and cinnamon. Leave them to rest while preparing the dough. All the ingredients for the dough should be mixed in a deep bowl. Brush a deep tray or a medium-sized baking dish with oil and dust with flour. Do not use a dish that is too large, as your crust may turn out too thin. Pour half of the mixture into the tray and bake until it hardens, for about 10 minutes at 360 F. The dough should not be completely baked. Pour the grated apples with their juices on the crust. Pour the remaining batter over the apples. Bake for about 30 minutes at 360 F, until it becomes nicely golden yellow.

Plum dumplings (Knedle sa shljivama)

Preparation time: 35 minutes
Cooking time: 35 minutes

Ingredients (5 servings)

15 plums
1 pound of peeled potatoes
1 teaspoon of butter
1 egg yolk
1 cup of soft flour
2 tablespoons of semolina
A pinch of salt
Flour for shaping the dumplings
½ pound of breadcrumbs
Oil or butter
1 tablespoon of vanilla sugar
Sugar to taste

Preparation

Cut the potatoes into smaller chunks and cook in boiling water. Once cooked, the potatoes should be drained and immediately mashed with butter. Leave them to cool and then add salt, semolina, egg yolk and flour. Knead the dough, dust the surface with flour and roll the dough. Cut it into 15 squares. Put a plum on each piece of the dough and form dumplings. Cook them in about 9 cups of boiling water with 1/2 a teaspoon of salt. Once the dumplings rise to the surface, cook them for a few more minutes. While the dumplings are cooking, prepare the breadcrumbs – fry them in hot oil until they are light golden. Use a slotted spoon to remove the dumplings from water and place them into the breadcrumbs. Finally, sprinkle them with vanilla sugar and sweeten with plain sugar according to your preference.

Rice pudding (*Sutlijaš*)

Preparation time: 15 minutes
Cooking time: 25 minutes

Ingredients (5 servings)
½ pound of rice
5 cups of milk
6 tablespoons of sugar
1 cup of raisins
1 package of vanilla sugar
Cinnamon

Preparation
Rinse the rice, add milk and cook at a low heat for up to 20 minutes. The rice pudding should be stirred regularly so that it does not burn. More milk or water can be added as needed and according to taste. Once the rice grains break and the dessert becomes creamy, add vanilla sugar, sugar, raisins and cook for a few more minutes. Pour into small bowls and sprinkle with cinnamon according to taste.

Meringue Slices (*Shampita*)

Preparation time: 45 minutes
Cooking time: 45 minutes

Ingredients (6 servings)
1 package (1 pound) of puff pastry (thawed)
8 large egg whites
1 1/3 cups of sugar
2 1/2 cups of water
Confectioners' sugar

Preparation

Heat the oven to 400 F. On a parchment-lined baking sheet, sandwich a puff pastry sheet (that has been pierced throughout with a fork) between two cooling racks. This will keep the pastry flat, but still flaky. Bake for 15 minutes or until golden, cool completely and repeat with the second puff pastry sheet.

In a medium saucepan, boil water and sugar without stirring for 7 minutes, until thick and syrupy. Do not touch the crystalized sugar on the sides of the pan with a mixing spoon. In a stand mixer or a heatproof bowl, beat the egg whites until stiff and very slowly pour the hot sugar syrup into the egg whites, beating constantly. After all the sugar syrup has been added, beat for another 6 minutes. Immediately pour the filling over one of the pastry layers. Place the other pastry layer on top and let it cool completely. Then refrigerate until ready to serve. Dust with confectioners' sugar.

Vanilla Slice (*Krempita*)

Preparation time: 20 minutes
Cooking time: 30 minutes

Ingredients (25 servings)
12 cups of milk
1 sachet of vanilla sugar
8 eggs
4/5 pound of sugar
½ pound of white flour
1 package of puff pastry sheets

Preparation
Spread the puff pastry sheets to form two identical dough sheets that fit the pan shape, and bake them in the oven separately. Before baking, make square slashes with a knife across the surface of the pastry sheet prepared for the upper crust to facilitate slicing. Prick the pastry sheet for the bottom crust all over with a fork to make sure that the crust doesn't puff.

Put the milk and a sachet of vanilla sugar into a saucepan and boil. Meanwhile, put 8 egg yolks and 2/3 pound of sugar in a separate saucepan and whisk, then add ½ pound of flour and stir with a wire whisk. Slowly pour the boiled milk over, stirring the mixture gently and constantly with a wire whisk. Steam the cream, stirring constantly. When it becomes thick, add the snow made from 6 beaten egg whites and 1 cup of sugar. Using a wire whisk, quickly stir the mixture well, remove the pan from the stove, pour cream over the bottom crust and spread, then cover it with the top crust. Leave it to cool, then cut a vanilla slice into square pieces and sprinkle with powdered sugar over the top.

Apricot cake

Preparation time: 20 minutes
Cooking time: 60 minutes

Ingredients

2 teaspoons of active dry yeast
⅛ cup of warm water
1/3 pound of softened butter
1¾ cups of plain flour
2 large eggs
¼ cup of sour cream
¾ cup of finely chopped walnuts/slivered almonds
½ rounded cup of sugar
½ teaspoon of cinnamon
½ cup of apricot jam or fresh apricot puree
¼ teaspoon of cream of tartar
¼ cup of castor sugar
¼ cup of flaked almonds/finely chopped walnuts

Preparation

Dissolve the yeast in ¼ cup of warm water in a small bowl and set aside. Grease a cake tin 10 x 6 x 1 1/3 inches deep. Heat oven to 360 F. In a processor or a mixer, blend the butter and flour. Mix the egg yolks, sour cream and add to the yeast. Add it all to the flour mixture and blend until a ball of dough forms, but do not knead. Divide the dough into 3 equal parts. On a lightly floured board, roll one part into a rectangle and place it in the prepared pan. In a medium bowl, mix the sugar, cinnamon and chopped nuts and sprinkle over the dough in the pan. Roll out the second piece of the dough and place it on top. Spread with apricot filling or jam. Roll out the remaining piece of the dough and place it on top. Bake for up to 50 minutes or until top is golden brown and is cooked. When almost ready, beat the egg whites until foamy. Add the cream of tartar and beat until soft peaks form. Add castor sugar gradually, beating until stiff peaks form. Remove the cake from the oven and spread the meringue over the top. Sprinkle with the remaining ¼ cup of the nuts. Bake until the meringue is golden and serve warm.

Serbian Honey Cookies (*Medenjaci*)

Preparation time: 20 minutes
Cooking time: 20 minutes

Ingredients (12 servings)

2 eggs
10 tablespoons of white sugar
7 tablespoons of honey
4 tablespoons of olive or vegetable oil
2 teaspoons of baking soda
Icing sugar for decoration
Plain flour
Salt

Preparation

Preheat the oven to 350 F. Beat the eggs in a bowl and add the sugar, honey, oil, baking soda and salt and mix. Slowly add the sifted flour bit by bit in order to get quite a sticky mixture. Flour hands so that the small pieces of the mixture can be rolled into balls (there should be around 22-24 pieces) and press down with hands to flatten. Place onto a baking tray that has been greased lightly and bake in the oven for 15 minutes. When ready take the baking tray out of the oven, allow them to sit for 10 minutes and sprinkle icing sugar on top.

Cherry Pie

Preparation time: 15 minutes
Cooking time: 30 minutes

Ingredients

4 eggs
1 ¼ cups of sugar
2 vanilla sugar
1 cup of oil
2 ½ cups of yogurt
1 ¾ pounds of flour
2 teaspoons of baking powder
1 jar of pitted cherries

Preparation

Mix together the eggs and sugar, gradually add the yogurt and oil. Add flour mixed with the baking powder. Mix everything together and pour in a buttered and floured baking dish. Place the well drained cherries (dense if possible) on top of the cake. Bake in a preheated oven at 330-360 F for 30 minutes, or until the cake becomes golden on top. Cool the cake and dust it with icing sugar on top.

Serbian Pumpkin Pie (*Bundevara*)

Preparation time: 50 minutes
Cooking time: 50 minutes

Ingredients (12 servings)
18 phyllo dough sheets
18 tablespoons of caster sugar
6 teaspoons of cinnamon
3 pounds of pumpkin, peeled and grated
½ cup of oil
For the garnishing
Sugar or icing sugar

Preparation
On a lightly oiled work surface, place a phyllo sheet, add a tablespoon of oil and spread it with a brush, then sprinkle the entire surface of the dough with a tablespoon of sugar. Place the second sheet on top and repeat the process with oil and sugar. Place the third sheet on top of the other two. Take ½ pound of grated pumpkin, spread evenly, leaving about 5 inches of space on one side. Sprinkle the pumpkin with a tablespoon of sugar and a teaspoon of cinnamon. Roll the pumpkin-filled sheets, starting from the empty side. Place the roll in a baking dish lined with a parchment paper. Repeat the process with the other sheets to obtain 6 more rolls. Brush all the rolls with oil. Preheat a convection oven to 350 F. Bake for 40-50 minutes. Remove the rolls from the oven, cover them with a damp cotton cloth and let cool. Slice the rolls, sprinkle with sugar or icing sugar and serve.

Japanese wind

Preparation time: 50 minutes
Cooking time: 50 minutes

Ingredients (5 servings)
4 egg whites
1/5 pound of margarine
½ pound of caster sugar
12 cupsnof milk
1/3 pound of walnuts
1 teaspoon of cider vinegar
4 egg yolks
½ pound of sugar
1/5 pound of strong flour
Whipped cream

Preparation
Preheat the oven to 300 F. Prepare the meringue by separating the eggs. Whip the egg whites into stiff peaks and add the vinegar and sugar gradually. Grease three Swiss roll tins and divide the mixture onto them equally. Bake in a preheated oven for 45-50 minutes. For the filling, use a mixer to combine the egg yolks and sugar, beating well. Sift the flour into the mix and keep beating so that there are no lumps left. Add the milk and stir the mixture thoroughly. When the mixture is without lumps, put it in a saucepan and stir over the heat until little bubbles form. Add a little lemon rind to taste. Add the margarine or butter into the warm mixture and stir until it has completely melted. When the mixture is cold, add the finely chopped walnuts. Whip the cream until it's softly thick, adding sugar if desired. Arrange in layers (meringue/filling/meringue/filling), cut into pieces and serve.

Serbian Dry Walnut Pie

Preparation time: 50 minutes
Cooking time: 30 minutes (plus 13 hours of cooling)

Ingredients (15 servings)

1 pound of ground walnuts

7 oz of raisins

8 oz plus 1 pound of sugar, separately

4 oz of oil

1 pound of phyllo pastry sheets, 14x16 inch

16 oz of water

1 lemon, thinly sliced with peel

Preparation

Mix together the walnuts, raisins, and 8 oz of sugar in a bowl. Place 1 sheet of phyllo dough in a deep-dish and sprinkle with oil. Repeat the process with two more layers like this. After the next phyllo, spread 4 tablespoons of the walnut mixture. Layer the phyllo on top and sprinkle with oil. Repeat this two more times. Add a layer with another 4-5 tablespoons of the walnut mixture. Continue layering, alternating the phyllo dough layers with oil and then the walnut layers, until all the walnut mixture is gone. The top has three phyllo sheets sprinkled generously with oil.

Preheat the oven to 375 F and cut the phyllo into inch size rectangles. Bake for 25-30 minutes or until golden brown. Add a pound of sugar to the water and boil it until the sugar dissolves and the mixture starts to become sticky. Then add the lemon slices. Slowly pour the warm mixture over the baked pie. Refrigerate overnight and cut into small pieces.

If you liked Serbian food, discover to how cook DELICIOUS recipes from other Balkan countries!

Within these pages, you'll learn 35 authentic recipes from a Balkan cook. These aren't ordinary recipes you'd find on the Internet, but recipes that were closely guarded by our Balkan mothers and passed down from generation to generation.

Main Dishes, Appetizers, and Desserts included!

If you want to learn how to make Croatian green peas stew, and 32 other authentic Balkan recipes, then start with our book!

Order <u>HERE</u> now for only $2,99

If you like Serbian food, but you're a Mediterranean dieter who wants to know the secrets of the Mediterranean diet, dieting, and cooking, then you're about to discover how to master cooking meals on a Mediterranean diet right now!

In fact, if you want to know how to make Mediterranean food, then this new e-book - "The 30-minute Mediterranean diet" - gives you the answers to many important questions and challenges every Mediterranean dieter faces, including:

How can I succeed with a Mediterranean diet?

What kind of recipes can I make?

What are the key principles to this type of diet?

What are the suggested weekly menus for this diet?

Are there any cheat items I can make?

... and more!

If you're serious about cooking meals on a Mediterranean diet and you really want to know how to make Mediterranean food, then you need to grab a copy of "The 30-minute Mediterranean diet" right now.

Prepare **111 recipes with several ingredients in less than 30 minutes!**

Order <u>HERE</u> now for only $2,99!

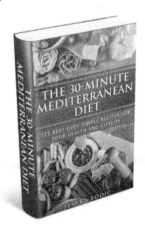

What could be better than a home-cooked meal? Maybe only a Greek homemade meal.

Do not get discouraged if you have no Greek roots or friends.

Now you can make a Greek food feast in your kitchen.

This ultimate Greek cookbook offers you 111 best dishes of this cuisine! From more famous gyros to more exotic Kota Kapama this cookbook keeps it easy and affordable.

All the ingredients necessary are wholesome and widely accessible.

The author's picks are as flavorful as they are healthy. The dishes described in this cookbook are "what Greek mothers have made for decades."

Full of well-balanced and nutritious meals, this handy cookbook includes many vegan options.
Discover a plethora of benefits of Mediterranean cuisine, and you may fall in love with cooking at home.

Inspired by a real food lover, this collection of delicious recipes will taste buds utterly satisfied.

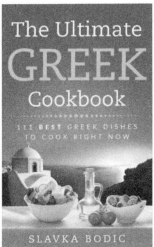

Order <u>HERE</u> now for only $2,99!

ONE LAST THING

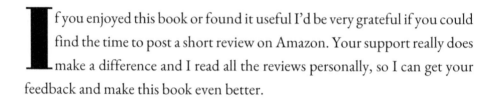

If you enjoyed this book or found it useful I'd be very grateful if you could find the time to post a short review on Amazon. Your support really does make a difference and I read all the reviews personally, so I can get your feedback and make this book even better.

Thanks again for your support!

Please send me your feedback at

www.balkanfood.org

Printed in Great Britain
by Amazon